HEBREW
FOR THE
REST OF US
WORKBOOK

HEBREW
FOR THE
REST OF US
WORKBOOK

USING HEBREW TOOLS TO STUDY
THE OLD TESTAMENT

LEE M. FIELDS

ZONDERVAN
ACADEMIC

ZONDERVAN ACADEMIC

Hebrew for the Rest of Us Workbook
Copyright © 2023 by Lee M. Fields

Requests for information should be addressed to:
Zondervan, *3900 Sparks Dr. SE, Grand Rapids, Michigan 49546*

Zondervan titles may be purchased in bulk for educational, business, fundraising, or sales promotional use. For information, please email SpecialMarkets@Zondervan.com.

ISBN 978-0-310-13614-9 (softcover)
ISBN 978-0-310-13615-6 (ebook)

Cover design: LUCAS Art & Design
Interior design: Kait Lamphere

Printed in the United States of America

23 24 25 26 27 28 29 30 31 32 33 34 35 36 37 38 /PHP/ 18 17 16 15 14 13 12 11 10 9 8 7 6 5 4 3 2 1

CONTENTS

Preface vii

Abbreviations ix

1. It Doesn't Look like Greek to Me 1
   The Hebrew Alphabet

2. Whose Language Is Dead? 7
   The History of Hebrew

3. Get the Point? 13
   The Hebrew Vowels

4. Tablets of Stone, Jars of Clay 19
   Canon, Text, and Versions

5. Getting to the Root of the Matter 25
   Hebrew Word Roots

6. Yes, Virginia, There Are 35
   Clauses

7. Wow! 41
   The Conjunction Waw and Friends

8. Let's Not Get Ourselves Ahead Of 47
   Prepositions

9. What's in a Name? 51
   Overview of Nominals

10. Be Sure You Read This! 53
    The Article

11. A Tale of Two States 57
    Case Functions

12. An Apt Description 71
    Adjectives

13. Where the Action Is 77
    Overview of Verbals

14. When the Perfect Comes 85
    Perfect Forms

15. There's Nothing Wrong with 89
    Imperfect Forms
16. Where There's a Will, There Are 93
    Volitional Forms
17. To Infinitives and Beyond! 99
    Infinitives & Participles
18. What Do You Mean? 103
    Hebrew Word Studies
19. Tools of the Trade 107
    Books in Paper and Electronic Form
20. If It's Not Poetry, It's 109
    Hebrew Prose
21. It May Not Rhyme, but It's Still 111
    Hebrew Poetry

Supplemental Helps 115
    1. *Keys to Reading Charts* 115
        Ch. 3, #1, Simple Vowels (Use as Key and for reading practice.) 115
        Ch. 4, #4, Composite Vowels (Use as Key and for reading practice.) 117
    2. *Flowcharting Keys* 118
        Ch. 6, Ex. 6 Keys 118
        Ch. 7, Ex. 6 Keys 123
        Ch. 12, Ex. 4 Keys 129
        Ch. 20, #2, Flowchart Keys 134
        Ch. 21, #3, Flowchart Keys 141

PREFACE TO THE WORKBOOK

Welcome to *Hebrew for the Rest of Us Workbook* (*HRUW*)!

Completing the activities in this workbook provides opportunity to practice the skills presented in *Hebrew for the Rest of Us*, second edition (*HRU2*). Trying to learn the content of *HRU2* without doing the exercises is like trying to learn to play baseball by only reading the rulebook.

The exercises in this book go far beyond those in the first edition of *HRU*. I produced more than some people might complete, but the more you practice, the better you get. The exercises are designed to be more easily gradable and more suitable for online learning. Some will be challenging, and some will be fun—well, that was my intention, anyway.

Of particular importance are the large charts in chs. 3 and 4. These take time to complete, but field testing done by some church friends revealed that completing these charts by hand helped them learn the material very well. A full key of these two charts is provided in the back of this workbook so you can grade yourself. They may also come in handy when you practice pronunciation.

How to Use This Book

1. **Get a study partner.** If you have at least one person to study with, you will find comparing answers to be encouraging and instructive. If you are in a college course or with worship friends, this is relatively easy. If you are studying alone, these days with internet connections, you are basically unlimited geographically in finding a partner.

2. **Read the chapter in *HRU2*.** Various options for the order and amount of reading are given in the preface to *HRU2*. When reading the text for content, take time to study the examples rather than merely skimming the examples. This will help you to understand the content better and to know how to do the exercises.

3. **Do the exercises in *HRUW* for the corresponding chapter in *HRU2*.** Each chapter in the *Workbook* has several exercises. Each exercise begins with at least one example to illustrate how to perform the exercise. Aim to do at least the half of the exercises skipping every other one (i.e., a, c, e, etc.). The more you practice, the faster you will become.

4. **Avail yourself of available resources.** In the back of the *Workbook* students will find some keys and some photocopiable pages. Audio files and other downloadable material may be freely accessed with an account under Instructor Resources at zondervanacademic.com.

5. **Use keys to check your answers to the "odd" exercises.** This is freely available with an account under Instructor Resources at zondervanacademic.com. If you are a professor, you could use the "odd" exercises for in-class activities and assign the "even" exercises for grading. Professors may register on the Zondervan website to access the full key for grading.

6. **Be satisfied with some ambiguity.** I've made an effort to make questions and answers unambiguous. Some matters, though, are interpretive and permit a latitude of response. This is part of the joy of interpretation! The exercises sometimes offer "suggested" answers. Feel free to disagree with me over some responses. This is where discussing matters with a partner can be fun.

Acknowledgments

I am thankful to the students in my classes at Mid-Atlantic Christian University and other individuals whose feedback has been invaluable in developing and improving the resources for *HRU* in general and the *Workbook* in particular. Thanks to Nancy Erickson for her longsuffering nature, to Kait Lamphere for her design skills, and especially to Michael Williams for his careful reading and invaluable suggestions. Of course, remaining errors are the responsibility of this author. May God bless us all as we seek to see both him and ourselves more accurately, so that we may become more like his Son (Rom 8:29).

נֵר־לְרַגְלִי דְבָרֶךָ וְאוֹר לִנְתִיבָתִי
—Psalm 119:105

ABBREVIATIONS

Bible Book Abbreviations

Gen	Genesis	Mic	Micah
Exod	Exodus	Nah	Nahum
Lev	Leviticus	Hab	Habakkuk
Num	Numbers	Zeph	Zephaniah
Deut	Deuteronomy	Hag	Haggai
Josh	Joshua	Zech	Zechariah
Judg	Judges	Mal	Malachi
Ruth	Ruth	Matt	Matthew
1–2 Sam	1–2 Samuel	Mark	Mark
1–2 Kgs	1–2 Kings	Luke	Luke
1–2 Chr	1–2 Chronicles	John	John
Ezra	Ezra	Acts	Acts
Neh	Nehemiah	Rom	Romans
Esth	Esther	1–2 Cor	1–2 Corinthians
Job	Job	Gal	Galatians
Ps (Pss)	Psalm(s)	Eph	Ephesians
Prov	Proverbs	Phil	Philippians
Eccl	Ecclesiastes	Col	Colossians
Song	Song of Songs/Solomon	1–2 Tim	1–2 Timothy
Isa	Isaiah	1–2 Thess	1–2 Thessalonians
Jer	Jeremiah	Titus	Titus
Lam	Lamentations	Phlm	Philemon
Ezek	Ezekiel	Heb	Hebrews
Dan	Daniel	Jas	James
Hos	Hosea	1–2 Pet	1–2 Peter
Joel	Joel	1–2–3 John	1–2–3 John
Amos	Amos	Jude	Jude
Obad	Obadiah	Rev	Revelation
Jonah	Jonah		

Version Abbreviations

ESV	English Standard Version	NCV	New Century Version
GNB	Good News Bible	NEB	New English Bible
JB	Jerusalem Bible	NET	New English Translation
KJV	King James Version	NIV	New International Version (2011)
LB	Living Bible	NIV84	New International Version (1984)
MSG	The Message	NLT	New Living Translation
NAB	New American Bible	NRSV	New Revised Standard Version
NASB	New American Standard Bible (1995 revision)	RSV	Revised Standard Version
		TEV	Today's English Version

Grammatical and General Abbreviations

(Not all of these are used in *HRU2*, but you may still find them helpful for your own study.)

1	first person	Dp	*pual* stem
2	second person	Emph	emphatic aspect
3	third person	f	feminine
A	active (used only in combinations)	Fut	future tense
Abs	absolute state	G	gender, *qal* stem (used by some; we use Q here)
Acc	accusative case		
Act	active	Gen	genitive case
Adj	adjective	H	*hiphil* stem
Adv	adverb	Hp	*hophal* stem
Ar	Aramaic	HtD	*hithpael* stem
Art	article	Imp	imperfect tense
BA	Biblical Aramaic	Imv	imperative mood
BH	Biblical Hebrew	Ind	indicative mood
BHQ	Biblia Hebraica Quinta	Inf	infinitive
BHS	Biblia Hebraica Stuttgartensia	InfA	infinitive absolute
c	common	InfC	infinitive construct
cj	conjunction/conjunctive	IO	indirect object
Coh	cohortative	Juss	jussive
cs	consecutive	Lex	lexical form
Cst	construct state	LXX	Septuagint
d	dual	m	masculine
D	*piel* stem	MnCl	main clause
Dat	dative case	n	neuter
Det	determined	N	*niphal* stem, Number
DO	direct object	Nl	nominal

Nn	noun		PtcP	participle passive
Nom	nominative case		PtSp	part of speech
NV	nonverb		Q	*qal*
OC	objective case		RC	relative clause
P	person		Reflex	reflexive
p	plural		RhQ	rhetorical question
Pass	passive		RPrn	relative pronoun
PC	possessive case		s	singular
Pf	perfect tense/aspect		S	subject (when an abbreviation shorter than Subj is needed)
PN	predicate nominative			
Pp	preposition		SbCl	subordinate clause
PPhr	prepositional phrase		Sbj	subjunctive mood
PPrn	personal pronoun		SC	subject case
Pr	present tense		Smpl	simple aspect
Pred	predicate		Subj	subject
Pref	prefix		Suff	suffix
Pret	preterite		T	article (when an abbreviation shorter than Art is needed)
Prg	progressive aspect			
Prn	pronoun		TA	Talmudic Aramaic
PrnSf	pronominal suffix		targ	targum
PrPtc	present participle		U	undetermined
Pst	past tense		V	verb
PstPtc	past participle		Va	verb active voice
Ptc	participle		Voc	vocative case
PtcA	participle active		Vp	verb passive voice

CHAPTER 1

IT DOESN'T LOOK LIKE GREEK TO ME

The Hebrew Alphabet

1. **Alphabet Song.** Learn to sing "The Hebrew *Aleph Bet*" song in appendix 1 to *Hebrew for the Rest of Us*.

2. **Letters**. Practice writing the Hebrew letters by following the directions below.
   a. *Trace* the printed strokes starting at the top.
   b. *Copy* the letters in the remaining space.
   c. *Repeat* the name of the letter aloud each time you write it (a rhyming English word is in italics below the name of each letter to indicate proper vowel sounds; accented syllables are underlined).

WRITING THE HEBREW LETTERS

Narrow Letters

yod
road

waw
suave

final nun
noon

nun

noon

zayin

buy in

gimel

dimple

(with no p)

Wide Letters

kapf

cough

pe

pay

final pe

pay

samek

saw deck

Note rounded sides

qoph

loaf

resh

ray + sh

Note flatter side

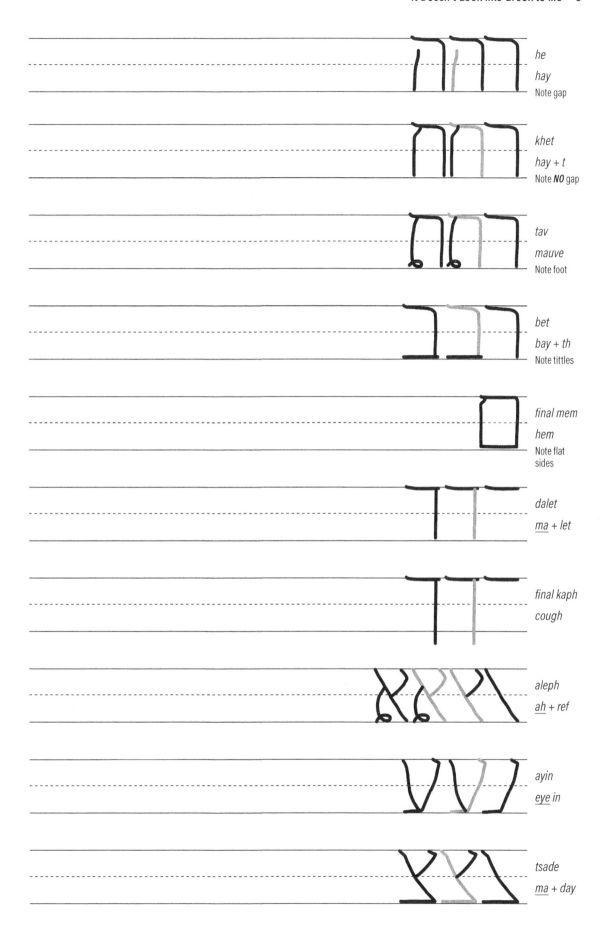

he

hay

Note gap

khet

hay + t

Note **NO** gap

tav

mauve

Note foot

bet

bay + th

Note tittles

final mem

hem

Note flat sides

dalet

ma + let

final kaph

cough

aleph

ah + ref

ayin

eye in

tsade

ma + day

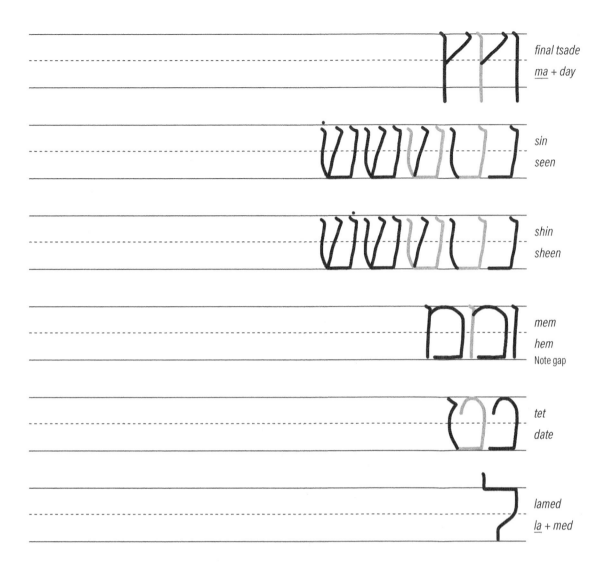

final tsade
_ma_ + day

sin
seen

shin
sheen

mem
hem
Note gap

tet
date

lamed
_la_ + med

3. **Alphabetical Order.** Write each letter of the entire alphabet once in alphabetical order, again naming the letter as you write. Include *begadkepat* letters and final forms. Complete the alphabet five times. The top lines are given as an example (Ex). After doing this for practice, you should doodle on your own whenever you have idle time; use unlined paper when possible.

ל	ד	כּ	כ	י	ט	ח	ז	ו	ה	דּ	ד	גּ	ג	בּ	ב	א	Ex
																	1
																	2
																	3
																	4
																	5

ת	ת	שׁ	שׂ	ר	ק	צ	פ	פ	פ	ע	ס	ן	נ	ם	מ	Ex
																1
																2
																3
																4
																5

4. **Transliteration.** Transliterate each of the following biblical names back into Hebrew letters. Can you figure out who or what they represent? You will need to supply the vowels in English. Try guessing first. If necessary, you may want to search in a Hebrew dictionary or a computer Bible.

Transliteration	Hebrew	English Name
Ex. *šlmh*	שלמה	Solomon
a. *byt lḥm*		
b. *rwt*		
c. *ʾbymlk*		
d. *dwd*		
e. *ʾbrm*		
f. *dnyyʾl*		
g. *bnymyn*		
h. *yḥzqʾl*		
i. *rḥl*		
j. *ʿzrʾ*		
k. *ʾstr*		
l. *hdssh*		

CHAPTER 2

WHOSE LANGUAGE IS DEAD?
The History of Hebrew

1. **Dagesh.** In the following words, some have *dagesh lene* (only in *begadkepat* letters), some have *dagesh forte* (marking the doubling of letters that may be found in almost any letter, including *begadkepat* letters), some have neither. Write the Hebrew letter in the column indicating whether the word has a *dagesh forte* or *dagesh lene*. If there is no *dagesh* at all, place an X in the last column. If there is more than one *dagesh* in a word, write each letter in the correct column. There are three examples.

Note: For this exercise, even though it will not be right, assume that all *begadkepat* letters have a *dagesh lene*.

	Word	*Dagesh Forte*	*Dagesh Lene*	No *Dagesh*
Ex. 1	ברא		ב	
Ex. 2	השׁמן	שׁ		
Ex. 3	אלהים			X
a.	תקחו			
b.	באהלו			
c.	מספר			
d.	לגלגלת			
e.	איש			
f.	ממנו			
g.	אשׁר			
h.	הדבר			
i.	ויבא			

(continued)

	Word	*Dagesh Forte*	*Dagesh Lene*	No *Dagesh*
j.	יְשַׁעְיָהוּ			
k.	הַנָּבִיא			
l.	דִּבְרַת			
m.	בִּשְׁלֹשׁ			
n.	וְדֶרֶךְ			
o.	יוֹדִיעֵנּוּ			

2. **Distinguishing Similar Letters.** Distinguish between similarly shaped letters by writing the letter in the "Answer(s)" column. If there are multiple answers, write them all. If there are no correct answers, write "none."

	Similar Letter Shapes	Which Letter Says[1]	Answer(s)
Ex.	א ב ג	/g/	ג
a.	פ ם ס	/s/	
b.	שׂ שׁ	/sh/	
c.	נ ו ג	/g/	
d.	י ו ן	/v/	
e.	ע א צ	/ts/	
f.	ח ת ה	/t/ or /th/	
g.	ב ב	/v/	
h.	ד ד ר	/d/	
i.	ע שׂ שׁ צ	/n/	
j.	ד ד ר	/r/	
k.	ס ם מ	/m/	
l.	ח ת ה	/ch/ as in Ba**ch**	
m.	י ו ן	/n/	
n.	ק כ ב פ	/k/	
o.	ע א צ	/silent/	

1. I'm using virgules to mark the sounds to distinguish from transliterations, which will be in another exercise; I am not using the technical sound symbols used in the International Phonetic Alphabet (IPA).

	Similar Letter Shapes	Which Letter Says[1]	Answer(s)
p.	ךזוף	/ph, f/	
q.	המחק	/h/	
r.	טפמ	/t/	
s.	ףצבפ	/ph, f/	

3. **Names and Transliterations.** In the chart below, draw lines from the letter in the center column to the correct names and transliterations. Each letter should have two lines, one extending from each of its circles. Answers may be used more than once or not at all. One is done as an example. If there is no correct answer, choose "[none]." The number of lines you draw will equal the number of circles in the center (Letter) column.

	Name	Letter	Transliteration
Ex.	aleph ○ bet ○ gimel ○ dalet ○	○ ג ○ ○ א ○ ○ ב ○	○ b ○ ḡ ○ ʿ ○ [none]
a.	aleph ○ tsade ○ shin ○ [none] ○	○ ע ○ ○ ט ○ ○ א ○	○ ʿ ○ ṭ ○ ʾ ○ [none]
b.	bet ○ final nun ○ gimel ○ [none] ○	○ ג ○ ○ ו ○ ○ נ ○	○ n ○ b̲ ○ w ○ g
c.	qoph ○ kaph ○ bet ○ [none] ○	○ פ ○ ○ ב ○ ○ כ ○	○ q ○ b ○ k̲ ○ p ○ [none]
d.	waw ○ final pe ○ final tsade ○ [none] ○	○ ף ○ ○ ד ○ ○ ו ○	○ n ○ p̄ ○ k̲ ○ [none]
e.	khet ○ waw ○ qoph ○ lamed ○	○ ל ○ ○ ו ○ ○ ק ○	○ k ○ w ○ l ○ q

(continued)

	Name	Letter	Transliteration
f.	final *tsade* ○		○ r
	kaph ○	○ ךּ ○	○ d̲
	final *pe* ○	○ ץ ○	○ k̲
	dalet ○	○ ף ○	○ ṣ
	[none] ○		○ p̄
g.			○ n
	bet ○	○ בּ ○	○ b̲
	kaph ○	○ ג ○	○ b
	waw ○	○ ב ○	○ ḡ
	gimel ○		○ [none]
h.	*aleph* ○		○ d̲
	tav ○	○ נ ○	○ r
	resh ○	○ ג ○	○ ḡ
	Gimel ○	○ ר ○	○ n
	[none] ○		○ w
i.	*he* ○		○ ḥ
	ayin ○	○ ח ○	○ h
	tav ○	○ ה ○	○ ś
	tet ○	○ ט ○	○ š
	[none] ○		○ t̲
j.	*yod* ○		○ r
	resh ○	○ י ○	○ d̲
	dalet ○	○ ד ○	○ ʾ
	ayin ○	○ א ○	○ y
	[none] ○		○ [none]
k.	*tav* ○		○ r
	khet ○	○ ד ○	○ ṭ
	qoph ○	○ ק ○	○ d̲
	resh ○	○ ת ○	○ t
	[none] ○		○ q
l.	*samek* ○		○ s
	ayin ○	○ שׂ ○	○ š
	final *tsade* ○	○ צ ○	○ ṣ
	shin ○	○ ס ○	○ ś
	tet ○	○ ץ ○	○ ṭ
	tav ○	○ שׁ ○	○ t
	sin ○	○ ט ○	○ t̲
	[none] ○		○ [none]

4. **Alphabetical Order.** For each group of letters, write in the blank the letter A, B, or C of the Hebrew letter that comes first alphabetically.

Ex. <u>A</u>   A. א   B. ר   C. ב

a. ___   A. ס   B. ן   C. שׁ

b. ___   A. מ   B. ע   C. ב

c. ___   A. ל   B. ע   C. נ

d. ___   A. פ   B. ט   C. ד

e. ___   A. ת   B. ט   C. ץ

f. ___   A. מ   B. כ   C. י

g. ___   A. כ   B. פ   C. ת

h. ___   A. ר   B. נ   C. ח

i. ___   A. ת   B. שׁ   C. שׂ

j. ___   A. כ   B. ר   C. ד

5. **Intervening Letters.** Write the letters that come between each pair of letters. Remember to write the Hebrew in order from right to left. If there are no intervening letters, write "[none]."

	Interval	Intervening Letters
Ex. 1	ה . . . א	ב ג ד
Ex. 2	ת . . . שׁ	[none]
a.	כ . . . ח	
b.	ר . . . צ	
c.	ג . . . א	
d.	ק . . . צ	
e.	נ . . . י	
f.	ס . . . נ	

(continued)

	Interval	Intervening Letters
g.	ק . . . ת	
h.	ו . . . י	
i.	ל . . . ס	
j.	ד . . . ט	

6. **Transliteration and Alphabetical Order.** Below are the words from Isa 66:17. For now, treat the *dagesh* in all the *begadkepat* letters as *lene* and all those in other letters as *forte* by writing the letter twice. So, ב = *b̲*, בּ = b, and טּ = *ṭṭ*. Below the Hebrew text, copy the Hebrew words in Hebrew. Below your copy of the Hebrew text, give a transliteration, remembering that English is transliterated from left to right. Finally, alphabetize the words in the verse by writing the number, 1–16, above each word in the first line to indicate the order. One word (the third in text order and the fourth in alphabetical order) is done as an example.

			4			
בְּתוֹךְ	אַחַד	אַחַר	הַגַּנּוֹת	אֶל	וְהַמִּטַּהֲרִים	הַמִּתְקַדְּשִׁים
			אֶל			
			'l			

יְהוָה	נְאֻם	יָסֻפוּ	יַחְדָּו	וְהָעַכְבָּר	וְהַשֶּׁקֶץ	הַחֲזִיר	בְּשַׂר	אֹכְלֵי

7. **Typing in Hebrew.** On a separate electronic document (Word works best for typing in Hebrew), type the Hebrew alphabet so that it appears as follows.

```
                                        א ב ג ד ה
                            א ב ג ד ה   ו ז ח ט י
                  ו ז ח ט י   כ ד ל מם נן
                  כ ד ל מם נן   ס ע פף צץ
          ק ר שׁ שׂ ת   ס ע פף צץ
          ק ר שׁ שׂ ת
```

CHAPTER 3

GET THE POINT?

The Hebrew Vowels

1. **Practicing Letters with Simple Vowels.**

   a. Complete the chart below by writing the names of the letters, then writing the letters with the vowels. Then write the transliteration of the syllable below the Hebrew. Several of the letters are done as examples. Note that in the final column (the one farthest left! ☺), written for you is the final silent *shewa* to close the syllable. You might do well to review the discussion of *qamets* and figure 3.5 in *HRU*.

   **Remember that Hebrew is always written from right to left and English transliteration is written from left to right.*

   b. After completing the chart, practice reading the Hebrew syllables aloud. You can read vertically or horizontally.

◌ֻ ◌ָ	א , ◌ֹ	◌ַ	◌ֹ	◌ִ	◌ֶ	◌ֵ	◌ְ	**Letter**
◌ְ							אֱ *ʾi*	*aleph*
◌ְ						בֵ *bē*		
◌ְ					גֶ *ḡe*			
◌ְ				דֻ *du*				
◌ְ			הֹ *hō*					
◌ְ		וַ *wa*	וֹ,וו *ô, wô*	וּ *wwu*				

(continued)

---

1. The syllable וּ does not occur. When the *waw* is doubled, however, the *qibbuts* can occur, as in יָצְוֻּנִי, *yoṣaw | wu | nî.*

13

◌ְ ◌ָ	א , ◌ָ	◌ֹ	◌ֹ	◌ִ	◌ֵ	◌ֶ	◌ִ	Letter
◌	זְ, זָ *zā*							
◌ חָ *ḥo*								
◌							ט *ṭi*	*tet*
◌						יְ *yē*		
◌					כְ *ke*			
◌				לְ *lu*				
◌			מֹ *mō*					
◌		נַ *na*						
◌	סָ, סָ *sā*							
◌ עֳ *'o*								
◌							פִ *p̄i*	*pe*
◌						צֵ *ṣē*		
◌					קֶ *qe*			
◌				רְ *ru*				
◌			שֹׂ, שֹׁ *śō*					
◌		שַׁ *ša*						
◌	תָ, תָ *t̄ā*							

2. **Identifying Open and Closed Syllables.** For each syllable (some of them are actually Hebrew words, but that is irrelevant for this exercise), identify whether the syllable is open or closed by marking the correct box.

	Syllable	Open	Closed		Syllable	Open	Closed
Ex.	מִן		X	Ex.	לְךֵ	X	
a.	אִישׁ			b.	פְּ		
c.	קְט			d.	נָיו		
e.	לֶה			f.	בְּנֵי		
g.	דָם			h.	יִ		
i.	אֶ			j.	עֲקֹב		
k.	אֲבִי			l.	אֲשֶׁר		
m.	שִׂי			n.	זֶ		
o.	רוּ			p.	רַע		
q.	תָּ			r.	זִכְ		
s.	מִיד			t.	לֹא		

3. **Identifying Dots in Letters.** For each Hebrew word indicate what kind of dot is in the letter or letters by writing that letter in the appropriate column. If there is no dot in a letter, write an X in the "None" column.

	Word	*Dagesh Forte*	*Dagesh Lene*	*Mappiq*	*Shureq*	**None**
Ex.	וַיֹּאמְרוּ	י			וּ	
a.	לְיִפְתָּח					
b.	מַדּוּעַ					
c.	עָבַרְתָּ					
d.	לְהִלָּחֵם					
e.	בִּבְנֵי־					

(continued)

	Word	Dagesh Forte	Dagesh Lene	Mappiq	Shureq	None
f.	עַמּוֹן					
g.	וְלָנוּ					
h.	לֹא					
i.	עִמְּךָ					
j.	וּבְנֵי					
k.	כִּי					
l.	וַיִּלְכֹּד					

4. **Identifying Simple *Shewa*.** Indicate whether each *shewa* in each word is vocal (V) or silent (S) by writing each letter with *shewa* in the proper box.

S	V	Word	
שׁ	לְ	לְרִישְׁתָּהּ	Ex.
		לְבָבְךָ²	g.
		מְצַוְּךָ	h.
		תִּשְׁמַע	i.
		וְלֹא	j.
		הִגַּדְתִּי	k.
		אַשְׁרֵי	l.

S	V	Word	
	מְ	מִמְּךָ	Ex.
		מִשְׁפְּחוֹת	a.
		מְקַקְטְלִים	b.
		וַיֹּאמְרוּ	c.
		הָלַכְתִּי	d.
		שָׁבְרָה	e.
		וַיֵּבְךְ	f.

5. **Typing Practice.** Reproduce the text below by typing the letters of the alphabet with each of the simple vowels. Each line alternates with the *dagesh*. Final letters are not included, since they are not followed by a vowel, except for final *kaph*, which can occur with the *qamets* (ך) and when vowelless always includes the *shewa* (ך).

**If along the way you learn little copying tricks to speed up the process, that is a good thing! Notice the Microsoft Word (MSWord) autonumbering in right-to-left mode will make the numbering go that way, too.

---

2. Hint: Why is there no *dagesh* in the final *kaph* (which can take a *dagesh*: ךּ)?

a. אַ בְ גַ דְ הֹ וְ זֹ חֹ טִ יֹ כַּ ךְ לַ מֶ נֵ סַ עָ פַ צֶ קָ רֹ שֶׁ שֵׂ תּ

b. אַ בֶ גֵ דֶ הֶ וֶ זֶ חֶ טֶ יֶ כֶּ ךְ לֵ מֶ נֶ סֶ עֶ פֵּ צֶ קֶ רֶ שֶׁ שֵׂ תֶּ

c. אֶ בֶ גֶ דֶ הֶ וֶ זֶ חֶ טִ יֶ כֶּ דְ לֶ מֶ נֶ סֶ עָ פֵ צֶ עֶ קֶ רֶ שֶׁ שֵׂ תֶּ

d. אַ בֶ גֵ דְ הֹ וְ זְ חֹ טִ יְ כַּ דְ לֹ מֶ נֶ סֶ עֶ פֶּ צֶ קֶ רֶ שֶׁ שֵׂ תּ

e. אַ בְ גַ דַ הֹ וְ זֹ חַ טִ יְ כַדְ לַ מַ נ סֶ עֶ פַ צֶ עֶ קַ רַ שֶׁ שַׂ ת

f. אָ בְ גְּ דָ הָ וְ זָ חָ טִ יָ כְדְּ לָ מָ נָ סָ עֶ פְּ עֶ צְ קָ רָ שָׁ שָׂ תָּ

g. אֹ בֹ גֹ דֹ הֹ וֹ זֹ חֹ טֹ יֹ כדְ לֹ מֹ נֹ סֹ עֹ פֹ צֹ קֹ רֹ שֹׁ שֹׂ ת

CHAPTER 4

TABLETS OF STONE, JARS OF CLAY

Canon, Text, and Versions

1. **Terms.** Briefly define the following terms:

   a. Autograph

   b. MT

   c. Version

   d. LXX

   e. Textual criticism

2. How would you explain to a group of Christians who have not read anything on the topic why English translations are so different?

3. **Review.** Write out the twenty-three names of the twenty-two letters of the Hebrew alphabet in alphabetic order. The name of the first letter is written for you; just continue from there.
   aleph,

4. **Practicing Letters with Composite Vowels.**

   a. Complete the chart below by writing the letters with the vowels. Then write the transliteration of the syllable below the Hebrew. Several of the letters are done as examples.

   b. After completing the chart, practice reading the syllables aloud. You may access the audio-visual file on the Instructor Resources tab for *Hebrew for the Rest of Us Workbook* at www.zondervan academic.com.

יִ	יֵ	יִ	וֹוּ	וֹ	הֹ	הֶ	הֵ	הָ
								אָה ʾâ
							בֵה bēh	
						גֶה geh		
					דֹה dōh			
				הֹו hô				
			וֹוּ wû					
		זִי zî						
	חֵי ḥê							
טֶי ṭey								
								יָה yâ
							כֶה kēh	
						לֶה leh		
					מֹה mōh			

---

1. The consonantal *waw* can also be doubled in this combination: וּו, -wwû (e.g., Gen 27:29).

◌ִי	◌ֵי	◌ִי	וֹ◌	וֹ◌	הֹ◌	הֶ◌	הֵ◌	הָ◌
				נוֹ *nô*				
			סוּ *sû*					
		עִי *î*						
	פֵּי *pê*							
צֵי *ṣey*								
								קָה *qâ*
							רֵה *rēh*	
						שֶׂה *śeh*		
					שֹׂה *šōh*			
			תוֹ *tô*					

5. **Pronunciation.** In each row place a mark in the box next to all the syllables that have the sound indicated. For this exercise, include the *khatef* vowels with the full vowels of their class. For vocal *shewa*, use the /ə/ sound as at the beginning of *banana*. The first one is done as an example.

Ex. f**a**ther	בָ ☒	בַ ☒	בוֹ □	בִי ☒	בְ □
a. th**ey**	בֵ □	בֶ □	בוֹ □	בִי □	בֶ □
b. mach**i**ne	בֹ □	בָת □	בוֹ □	בִי □	בָ □
c. h**o**le	בֵ □	בוּ □	בָ □	בָת □	בִי □
d. th**ey**	בֶ □	בַ □	בֶ □	בִי □	בִי □
e. br**u**te	בֶ □	בַ □	בָ □	בוּ □	בֵ □

(continued)

f. hole	בֹּ □	בוּ □	בָ □	בָּגַ □	בַ □
g. brute	בְ □	בוּ □	בִּי □	בִּי □	בֵ □
h. machine	בִּי □	בֵ □	בֹ □	בֶ □	בֵ □
i. father	בָּתָ □	בַּת □	בוֹ □	בָ □	בֵ □
j. banana	בְ □	בוּ □	בְ □	בַ □	בֵ □

6. **Identifying Dots in Letters.** For each Hebrew word indicate what kind of dot is in the letter or letters by writing that letter in the appropriate column. If there is no dot in a letter, write an X in the "None" column.

	Word	Dagesh Forte	Dagesh Lene	Mappiq	Shureq	None
Ex.	וַיֹּאמְרוּ	י			וּ	
a.	וַיְהִי					
b.	בַּיּוֹם					
c.	הַשְּׁלִישִׁי					
d.	וְהִנֵּה					
e.	בָּא					
f.	הַמַּחֲנֶה					
g.	שָׁאוּל					
h.	וּבְגָדָיו					
i.	רֹאשׁוֹ					
j.	בְּבֹאוֹ					
k.	אֶל־דָּוִד					
l.	וַיִּפֹּל					
m.	וַיִּשְׁתַּחוּ					
n.	מִזֶּה					
o.	תָּבוֹא					

7. **Guess the Names.** Here are some Hebrew names of people and places. First give an accurate transliteration and then give the name as we normally spell it. The first one is done as an example. All words not accented on the last syllable are marked with the accent.

	Word	Transliteration	English Name
Ex.	רָחָב	*rāḥāḇ*	Rahab
a.	בֵּית לֶחֶם		
b.	יְרוּשָׁלַ͏ִם		
c.	נָעֳמִי²		
d.	יְהוּדָה		
e.	גָּלְיָת		
f.	דָּוִד		
g.	יְהוֹשָׁפָט		
h.	בַּת שֶׁבַע		
i.	שָׁאוּל		
j.	בָּבֶל		
k.	חִזְקִיָּהוּ		
l.	יוֹסֵף		

8. **Reading transliterations.** For the first six Hebrew words, select the correct transliteration. Then for the six transliterations, select the correct Hebrew word. (Recommended scoring: 5 pts for the correct answer, 4 pts for runner-up, etc.)

___ a. וַיְבָרֶךְ

  A. *waybāḏek*

  B. *waybārek*

  C. *gôyîm*

  D. *wəʾēleh*

  E. *bayyəkodek*

___ b. אֱלֹהִים

  A. *ʾĕlōhîm*

  B. *ʾĕluhîm*

  C. *ṣēriyyô*

  D. *ʾăloḥayim*

  E. *wəlōʾhîs*

---

2. The *qamets* before the *khatef qamets* is always *qamets hatuf* (o-class). In the English form of this name, the Hebrew o-class vowel is rendered with an English a-class vowel.

___ c. אֶת־נֹחַ

A. ʾeḥ-wuāṯ

B. ʾeṯ-nōah

C. ʾaṯ-gōḥ

D. ben-ṣērēy

E. ʾeṯ-nōaḥ

___ d. וַיֹּאמֶר

A. wayyōmer

B. wayyōʾmer

C. wattōʾmeḏ

D. waśśōmer

E. bəyedkem

___ e. לָהֶם

A. lāḥem

B. ʾăšer

C. lohas

D. qāḥin

E. lāhem

___ f. וּמִלְאוּ

A. wəšinʿu

B. ûmilʾû

C. wəḵiləû

D. ômilʾô

E. hāʾăḏāmâ

___ g. remes

A. רֶמֶס

B. לִדֹרת

C. רֶמָם

D. דֶּמֶס

E. דֶּמֶס

___ h. ləʾoklâ

A. לְעָכְל

B. לְעָבְדָה

C. לְאָכְלָה

D. לֶעָבְלָה

E. בְּעָנָן

___ i. nāṯattî

A. וְנִרְאֶתָה

B. נָתַתִּי

C. גֶּחַתִּי

D. וְתַטִּי

E. נָתֶתִּי

___ j. minnəʿurāyw

A. מִנְעָרִיו

B. מִנְאָרִיו

C. מִדְעָדִיו

D. מְנָאֲרִיה

E. לִשָׁחֶת

___ k. zeraʿ

A. נֵדַע

B. חַיַּת

C. זֵרָא

D. זֶרַע

E. זְדָא

___ l. bəkol-bāśār

A. רָצֶב־לְכָב

B. כְּבָל־כָּסָר

C. בֵּינִי

D. בְּכָל־בְּשָׂר

E. בְּכָל־בְּשַׂר

CHAPTER 5

GETTING TO THE ROOT OF THE MATTER

Hebrew Word Roots

1. **Review.** If you wish, you may sing the *aleph bet* song as a refresher on the names of the letters. In the exercise below, write the Hebrew letters of the alphabet and their transliterations. Include the *begadkepat* letters and final forms. Below each letter (L) write the transliteration (T).

															א	L
															ʼ	T

															L
															T

2. **Reading Practice.** The chart below gives lists of common Hebrew words of increasing numbers of syllables. Simple translations are provided simply to satisfy the curious. It is useful to do the exercise with a teacher or fellow student. See how quickly you can read each column. Remember that proper nouns are determined just as much as common nouns with the Art or nouns in construct with a determined noun. You may see the definite article in English translations even if there is no Art present in Hebrew. Remember, as mentioned in How to Use This Book, that, for each exercise labeled Reading Practice, you may access the audio-visual file on the Instructor Resources tab for *Hebrew for the Rest of Us Workbook* at www.zondervanacademic.com.

	1		2		3+	
a.	מִן	from	אָמַר	he said	וַיִּקְרָא	and he called
b.	עַל	upon	הָיָה	he was	וַיֹּאמֶר	and he said

(continued)

	1		2		3+	
c.	אֶל־	to	עָשָׂה	he did	זָכְרֵנִי	remember me
d.	כֹּל	all	מֶלֶךְ	king	מִפְּלִשְׁתִּים	from the Philistines
e.	לֹא	no, not	אֱלֹהִים	God, gods	הַמֵּתִים	the dead
f.	בֵּן	son	אֶרֶץ	land	וַיֵּרְדוּ	and they went down
g.	כִּי	for	בַּיִת	house	אֶשְׁתָּאֹל	Eshtaol
h.	אֲשֶׁר	which	פָּנִים	face	יִשְׂרָאֵל	Israel
i.	בּוֹא	to come	נָתַן	he gave	הִקְדַּשְׁתִּי	I sanctified
j.	יוֹם	day	הָלַךְ	he walked	מִמִּשְׁפַּחַט	from the family of
k.	שְׁמַע	hear!	אֶחָד	one	אֱלֹהֵינוּ	our God
l.	אֵת	[none]	וְהָיוּ	and they will be	וְאָהַבְתָּ	and you shall love
m.	בְּכָל־[1]	with all of	לְבָבְךָ	your heart	מְאֹדֶךָ	your strength

3. **Transliterating and Counting Syllables.** Indicate the syllables in each word by transliterating each Hebrew word and drawing a vertical line between syllables.

	Word	Transliteration		Word	Transliteration
Ex.	מְדַבְּרִים	məḏab | bərîm[2]	k.	וּשְׁנַיִם	
a.	לִיפְתָּח		l.	וַיִּשְׁפֹּט	
b.	מַדּוּעַ		m.	אַחֲרָיו	
c.	דִּבְרֵי		n.	עַבְדּוֹן	
d.	יֶלֶד		o.	וַיָּמָת	
e.	בְּרֵאשִׁית		p.	אֶפְרַיִם	
f.	אֱלֹהִים		q.	וְאִשְׁתּוֹ	
g.	שָׁלוֹחַ		r.	וּמוֹרָה	

---

1. The *maqqef* (Hebrew hyphen) at the end of בְּכָל־ means that the vowel syllable is closed and unaccented. This word would be transliterated *bəkol*. Please pronounce accordingly.

2. The *dagesh* is *forte*. Since the first ב concludes the syllable, I underlined it as aspirated; the second ב begins the syllable and is plosive, so it's not underlined. I did this for teaching purposes. If I were simply transliterating, I would not do this, and it would be *məḏabbərîm*. With the separation of syllables, the underlining makes sense.

	Word	Transliteration
h.	יִשְׂרָאֵל	
i.	נַעֲשֶׂה	
j.	הַגִּידוּ	

	Word	Transliteration
s.	פְּלִשְׁתִּים	
t.	הָאֱלֹהִים	
u.	יוֹשֶׁבֶת	

4. **Just for fun.** In the chart below are transliterations of English words into Hebrew. The goal is to practice pronouncing and then self-check by recognizing the intended English word. Please note: these transliterations have no connection to Hebrew words or meaning; this is simply a fun pronunciation exercise. Three words are real Hebrew words. Can you find them? At the end there is space for you to write to make up your own words in Hebrew letters and vowels for others to read. See if they can figure out what you are trying to write.

	Transliteration	English Word
Ex.	כּוֹט	coat
a.	פָּל	
b.	רֵיךְ	
c.	דָּג	
d.	הַלְלוּיָהּ	
e.	שׁוּא	
f.	פָּק	
g.	גּוֹלְד	
h.	כֵּר	
i.	תֵּרֵין	
j.	פִּיס	
k.	פְּלֶנט סתוֹנז	
l.	פִּית	

	Transliteration	English Word
m.	הִיבְּרוּ	
n.	גֶּם	
o.	פֵּז	
p.	אָמֵין	
q.	ברק	
r.	לֵג	
s.	מַת	
t.	עִיר	
u.	סֶל פוֹן	
v.	בִּיבֶּל	
w.	נוּ יוֹרק	
x.	ברד	
y.	עִמָּנוּאֵל	

5. **Figuring out Hebrew words from general-style transliterations.** Many commentaries, especially those written at a more popular level, use simplified systems of transliteration. In this exercise I will give you some samples from various commentaries and other reference books.[3] Your task is to identify

---

3. Please note that this exercise is not meant to denigrate any reference work. The use and style of transliteration depends largely on the intended readership and the expense. Resources used are DSB = Daily Study Bible series; HCBD = HarperCollins Bible Dictionary; FSB = Faithlife Study Bible; SRB = Scofield Reference Bible; CSBSB = CSB Study Bible; NIVCBSB = NIV Cultural Backgrounds Study Bible; LBD = Lexham Bible Dictionary; HBD = Harper's Bible Dictionary.

the Hebrew word by typing the Hebrew and giving the Strong's and G/K numbers. To do this, you will have to make your best guess for ambiguous letters and look them up in an exhaustive concordance that includes a lexicon (the *Strongest NIV Exhaustive Concordance* by Zondervan is recommended) or a wordbook. If you have Logos Bible Software, searching in the *Dictionary of Biblical Languages: Hebrew* will be quite efficient.

	General Transliteration	Resource	Hebrew	Strong's #	G/K #
Ex.	ʾadon	Young, *Isaiah*	אָדוֹן	113	123
a.	almah	DSB			
b.	betulah	DSB			
c.	kasdim	HCBD			
d.	achimelekh	LBD			
e.	kelalah	HBD			
f.	qatsaph	CSBSB			
g.	chesed	CSBSB			
h.	hartummim	NIVCBSB			
i.	elohim	FSB			
j.	Elyon	SRB			

6. **Finding Roots.** Using the *SNIVEC* or a computer Bible with this capability (see *HRU2*, ch 5. for this), find the roots to the following nouns. For each word give a definition, its G/K number, the G/K number of the root and a gloss. The first one is done as an example.

	Word	Definition	G/K#	G/K# of √	Gloss of √
Ex.	אַדֶּרֶת	cloak	168	158	make glorious
a.	טְרֵפָה				
b.	טְמֵאָה				

	Word	Definition	G/K#	G/K# of √	Gloss of √
c.	קָדַשׁ				
d.	תּוֹדָה				
e.	מֶרְכָּבָה				
f.	מִשְׁפָּט				
g.	דֶּרֶךְ				
h.	מִשְׁכָּן				
i.	מָשָׁל				
j.	מִשְׁמָר				

7. **Meanings of Names.** Proper names in the OT are often combinations of words, frequently words referring to God. The *SNIVEC* defines the names for you.[4]

If you have the *SNIVEC*, verify its definitions: (1) copy the name in Hebrew, (2) write the G/K number of the name, (3) write the name's definition in the *SNIVEC* lexicon, (4) list the G/K numbers of each component of the name, and (5) below each component write the definition.

If you have Logos, use the Bible Word Study feature to get links to resources and to roots. Under each root, find the matching word for numbers. Answers may vary depending on definitions given.

The definitions below come from the *Strong's Exhaustive Concordance* dictionary, because it is widely available, and I am using Strong's numbers. Newer scholarship may have different answers; G/K numbers are more precise and given in parentheses. Your teacher may or may not want to you give both. An example is given for you.

---

4. Other resources that give the meaning of names are *The Dictionary of Classical Hebrew* (*DCH*), Brown-Driver-Briggs (*BDB*), Gesenius' Hebrew-Chaldee Lexicon to the Old Testament, *The Hebrew and Aramaic Lexicon of the Old Testament* (*HALOT*), NASB Hebrew-Aramaic and Greek Dictionaries, *Enhanced Strong's Lexicon* (*ESL*), etc.

	English	Hebrew	Name Str# + Definition	Parts G/K# + Definitions
Ex.	Abram	אַבְרָם	87 (92), high father	1 (3), father 7311 (8123), to be high
a.	Abigail			1 (3), father
b.	Abimelek			1 (3), father
c.	Melchizedek			
d.	Zedekiah			
e.	Joel			
f.	Elijah			
g.	Isaiah			
h.	Hoshaiah			
i.	Joshua			
j.	Abidan			
k.	Daniel			
l.	Merib-Baal			
m.	Kirjath Baal			

	English	Hebrew	Name Str# + Definition	Parts G/K# + Definitions
n.	Jerubbesheth			
o.	Ish-Bosheth			
p.	Reuel			
q.	Reuben			
r.	Jeroboam			
s.	Ammiel			
t.	Benjamin			
u.	Benammi			
v.	Benaiah			
w.	Ezekiel			
x.	Hezekiah			
y.	Bethlehem			
z.	Beth Shemesh			

8. **Word Plays.** Explain the wordplay of the bolded words in each verse below: (1) copy the words in Hebrew as they appear in the Hebrew Bible and with transliteration, (2) give the G/K and Strong's numbers, and (3) write the G/K numbers for the roots. Then explain the wordplay. You may check your work by seeing if your Bible has a footnote explaining the play. For confirmation, see the notes in the NET Bible (available online at http://www.bible.org/netbible). Follow the example of Jer 1:11–12 given in ch. 5 of *HRU2*. You may write your own explanations, use commentaries, or both. The answer keys provide suggested explanations.

   a. That is why it was called **Babel**—because there the LORD **confused** the language of the whole world. (Gen 11:9 NIV)

NIV	Hebrew Text	G/K#	Gloss	G/K# of √	Str#
Babel					
confused					
Explanation:					

   b. Adam and his wife were both **naked**, and they felt no shame. Now the serpent was more **crafty** than any of the wild animals the LORD God had made. (Gen 2:25–3:1a NIV)

NIV	Hebrew Text	G/K#	Gloss	G/K# of √	Str#
naked					
crafty					
Explanation:					

   c. But Jonah ran away from the LORD and headed for Tarshish. **He went down** to Joppa, where he found a ship bound for that port. After paying the fare, **he went aboard** and sailed for Tarshish to flee from the LORD. (Jonah 1:3 NIV)

NIV	Hebrew Text	G/K#	Gloss	G/K# of √	Str#
he went down					
he went aboard					
Explanation:					

d. Then the LORD sent a great wind on the sea, and such a violent storm arose that the ship **threatened to break up**. (Jonah 1:4 NIV)

NIV	Hebrew Text	G/K#	Gloss	G/K# of √	Str#
threatened					
to break up					
Explanation:					

e. All the sailors were afraid and each cried out to his own god. And they threw the cargo into the sea to lighten the ship. But Jonah **had gone below** deck, where he lay down and **fell into a deep sleep**. (Jonah 1:5 NIV)

NIV	Hebrew Text	G/K#	Gloss	G/K# of √	Str#
had gone below					
fell into a deep sleep					
Explanation:					

f. "Don't call me Naomi," she told them. "Call me **Mara**, because the Almighty **has made my life** very **bitter**." (Ruth 1:20 NIV)

NIV	Hebrew Text	G/K#	Gloss	G/K# of √	Str#
Mara					
has made my life … bitter					
Explanation:					

g. The second son he named **Ephraim** and said, "It is because God **has made** me **fruitful** in the land of my suffering." (Gen 41:52 NIV)

NIV	Hebrew Text	G/K#	Gloss	G/K# of √	Str#
Ephraim					
has made … fruitful					
Explanation:					

h. So in the course of time Hannah became pregnant and gave birth to a son. She named him **Samuel**, saying, "Because **I asked** the Lord for him." (1 Sam 1:20 NIV)

NIV	Hebrew Text	G/K#	Gloss	G/K# of √	Str#
Samuel					
I asked					
Explanation:					

i. The man said, "This is now bone of my bones and flesh of my flesh; she shall be called '**woman**,' for she was taken out of **man**." (Gen 2:23 NIV)

NIV	Hebrew Text	G/K#	Gloss	G/K# of √	Str#
woman					
man					
Explanation:					

j. And the Lord God said, "The man has now become like one of us, knowing good and evil. He must not be allowed **to reach out** his hand and take also from the tree of life and eat, and live forever." So the Lord God **banished** him from the Garden of Eden to work the ground from which he had been taken. (Gen 3:22–23 NIV)

NIV	Hebrew Text	G/K#	Gloss	G/K# of √	Str#
to reach out					
banished					
Explanation:					

CHAPTER 6

YES, VIRGINIA, THERE ARE. . .
Clauses

1. **Review of Transliteration and Syllabification.** For each word below write a transliteration into Hebrew or into English, as is appropriate. Include syllable division in both cases. Two examples have been given.

Hebrew		Transliteration
הָאָ֫רֶץ	Ex.	hā | ʾā | reṣ
לְדָוִד	a.	
לֹא	b.	
יַרְבִּיצֵ֫נִי	c.	
מֵי	d.	
מִזְמוֹר	e.	
דֶּ֫שֶׁא	f.	
מְשָׁ | רֶת	Ex.	məšārēṯ
	g.	ʿal
	h.	rōʾî
	i.	mənuḥôṯ
	j.	ʾeḥsār
	k.	yənahălēnî
	l.	binəʾôṯ

35

2. **Typing Practice.** On a separate document type each of the Hebrew words in exercise 1, including the examples. Do not include the syllable dividers. If you want to be advanced, figure out how to add the accent mark (ʿ) for the three words from the first half of the list.

3. **Reading Practice.** Below is Ps 23:1–2 with the lines broken up at logical breaks. The NIV is provided in parallel. Notice that the first two words are the ancient Hebrew psalm title, and not part of the psalm itself. The NIV does not number this as a verse and places it in italic type. The Hebrew does include the title as part of the verse enumeration. I have replaced all the Masoretic accents with the ʿ accent. Practice reading this several times. You will develop muscle memory to read more smoothly. You may access the audio-visual file on the Instructor Resources tab for *Hebrew for the Rest of Us Workbook* at www.zondervanacademic.com.

מִזְמוֹר לְדָוִד יְהוָה רֹעִי לֹא אֶחְסָר:	1	*A psalm of David.* The Lᴏʀᴅ is my shepherd, I lack nothing.
בִּנְאוֹת דֶּשֶׁא יַרְבִּיצֵנִי עַל מֵי מְנֻחוֹת יְנַהֲלֵנִי:	2	He makes me lie down in green pastures, he leads me beside quiet waters,

4. **Key Root in a Passage.** For this exercise you will study 1 Sam 25 using the NASB. Find all of the words coming from the root made from the same three letters נבל in order. Remember that resources may number homonyms differently. The key and the example below, no. 1, follow the enumeration in *DBLH*. You may use the *SNIVEC* or *DBLH* in Logos. If using Logos, in Visual Filters » Resource » Corresponding Words, check all four boxes (same word, surface text, lemma, and root). In Logos interlinear, check surface, lemma (transliterated), root (transliterated), and Strong's number. Give this information for the following words. Words 4–9 are not found in 1 Sam 25 but are homophonic roots of the three words found in the chapter.

	Word (NASB)	LEMMA Translit.	ROOT G/K#	Str #	Translit.	G/K #	Str #
1.	Nabal (man's name)	*nābāl 2*	5573	5037	*nbl 2*	5573	5037
2.	folly, disgraceful thing (v. 25)						
3.	jugs (v. 18, "skins" in NIV)						
4.	wither, wear out						
5.	play the fool, dishonor						
6.	foolish, fool						
7.	harp						
8.	dead body						
9.	female private parts						

Drawing Conclusions:

    a. Discuss the wordplay in 1 Sam 25 and explain Abigail's comment in 1 Sam 25:25.

    b. How many different Hebrew words are translated "jug" in the NASB? ____

    c. Do you think the author's use of one of these words in v. 18 is meant to make a point, or is it just coincidental? If you think it is meant to make a point, what is its significance?

5. **Verbless Clauses.** For this exercise you will need to consult an interlinear Bible. For the verses below determine whether the clause is verbal, verbal with a form of הָיָה, or verbless by writing the verb or verb phrase in the correct column. Three are done as examples.

	Passage (NASB)	Verbal	הָיָה	Verbless
Ex. 1	In the beginning God created the heavens and the earth. (Gen 1:1)	created		
Ex. 2	The earth was formless and void (Gen 1:2a)		was	
Ex. 3	and darkness was over the surface of the deep (Gen 1:2b)			was
a.	while I was by the river Chebar among the exiles (Ezek 1:1a)			
b.	the heavens were opened (Ezek 1:1b)			
c.	and I saw visions of God. (Ezek 1:1c)			
d.	The word of the LORD came expressly to Ezekiel the priest (Ezek 1:3a)			
e.	and there the hand of the LORD came upon him. (Ezek 1:3b)			
f.	Now Deborah, a prophetess, the wife of Lappidoth, was judging Israel at that time. (Judg 4:4)			

(continued)

	Passage (NASB)	Verbal	הָיָה	Verbless
g.	She used to sit under the palm tree of Deborah between Ramah and Bethel in the hill country of Ephraim; (Judg 4:5a)			
h.	and the sons of Israel came up to her for judgment. (Judg 4:5b)			
i.	Now she sent (Judg 4:6a)			
j.	and summoned Barak the son of Abinoam from Kedesh-naphtali, (Judg 4:6b)			
k.	and said to him, (Judg 4:6c)			
l.	Behold, the Lord, the God of Israel, has commanded, (Judg 4:6d)			
m.	'Go (Judg 4:6e)			
n.	and march to Mount Tabor, (Judg 4:6f)			
o.	and take with you ten thousand men from the sons of Naphtali and from the sons of Zebulun. (Judg 4:6g)			
p.	'I will draw out to you Sisera, the commander of Jabin's army, with his chariots and his many *troops* to the river Kishon, (Judg 4:7a)			
q.	and I will give him into your hand.'" (Judg 4:7b)			

6. **Beginning Flowcharting.** On a separate sheet of paper (or e-paper ☺), make a flowchart for each of the passages below. For best results, use a word processor. You may prepare your own charts or download the form from the site mentioned in the introduction to the book. Be sure to keep all clause elements on the same line, indent subordinate clauses, and indent all modifiers either above or below the word they modify (don't worry about "Function" for now). If you wish, you may mark Subj, V, IO, and DO in some way: in the key to ch. 6, exercise 6, at the end of this book, I've **bolded** Subj, marked DO with an arrow (↓), and separated IO and V. I've added a column on the right to give a count of the number of clauses in the verse. Genesis 1:1 is done as an example. To maintain pagination with the *Workbook*, all the keys are at the end. Items a.–d. are simple ones to get you started.

Function	Vs	Gen 1:1 (NIV)		Ct
		In the beginning		1
	1	**God** created	→ the heavens	
			and	
			→ the earth.	

a.   I will break down the gate of Damascus. . . . (Amos 1:5a NIV)

b.   And I gave them to him. . . . (Mal 2:5b NIV)

c.   I gave you empty stomachs in every city. . . . (Amos 4:6a NIV)

d.   David took his men with him and . . . killed two hundred Philistines. (1 Sam 18:27a NIV)

2 Samuel 7:8c–16 (NASB)

e.   [8] I took you from the pasture, from following the sheep, to be ruler over My people Israel.

f.   [9] I have been with you wherever you have gone and have cut off all your enemies from before you; and I will make you a great name, like the names of the great men who are on the earth.

g.   [10] I will also appoint a place for My people Israel and will plant them, that they may live in their own place and not be disturbed again, nor will the wicked afflict them any more as formerly, [11] even from the day that I commanded judges to be over My people Israel; and I will give you rest from all your enemies.

h.   The LORD also declares to you that the LORD will make a house for you.

i.   [12] "When your days are complete and you lie down with your fathers, I will raise up your descendant after you, who will come forth from you, and I will establish his kingdom.

j.   [13] He shall build a house for My name, and I will establish the throne of his kingdom forever.

k.   [14] I will be a father to him and he will be a son to Me; when he commits iniquity, I will correct him with the rod of men and the strokes of the sons of men, [15] but My lovingkindness shall not depart from him, as I took *it* away from Saul, whom I removed from before you.

l.   [16] "Your house and your kingdom shall endure before Me forever; your throne shall be established forever.

CHAPTER 7

WOW!

The Conjunction *Waw* and Friends

1. **Review: Accent Recognition.** For each of the words below write the letter or letters that have an accent mark. If there is none, write an em dash (—) in the box. Distinguishing accents from vowels helps you gain recognition of what marks are in a printed Hebrew Bible. The words are taken from 1 Sam 16:6–7. One example is done. Once completed, you can practice reading aloud. For words with more than one accent, stress the final accented syllable. Access the audio-visual file at www.zondervanacademic.com.

	Word	Label
	אֲבִינָדָב ב, ד	Ex.
	וַיֵּרָא	c.
	וַיֹּאמֶר	f.
	יְהוָה	i.
	יְהֹוָה	l.
	אֶל־	o.
	מַרְאֵהוּ	r.
	קוֹמָתוֹ	u.
	כִּי	x.
	יִרְאֶה	aa.
	הָאָדָם	dd.
	וַיהוָה	gg.

	Word	Label
	וַיְהִי	a.
	אֶת־	d.
	אַךְ	g.
	מְשִׁיחוֹ:	j.
	אֶל־	m.
	תֵּבֵט	p.
	וְאֶל־	s.
	כִּי	v.
	לֹא	y.
	הָאָדָם	bb.
	יִרְאֶה	ee.
	יִרְאֶה	hh.

	Word	Label
	בְּבוֹאָם	b.
	אֱלִיאָב	e.
	נֶגֶד	h.
	וַיֹּאמֶר	k.
	שְׁמוּאֵל	n.
	אֶל־	q.
	גָּבְהַ	t.
	מָאַסְתִּיהוּ	w.
	אֲשֶׁר	z.
	כִּי	cc.
	לְעֵינַיִם	ff.
	לְלֵבָב:	ii.

2. **Reading Practice.** Below is Ps 23:3–4 with the lines broken up at logical breaks. The NIV is provided in parallel.

נַפְשִׁי יְשׁוֹבֵב יַנְחֵנִי בְמַעְגְּלֵי־צֶדֶק לְמַעַן שְׁמוֹ׃	3	he refreshes my soul. He guides me along the right paths for his name's sake.
גַּם כִּי־אֵלֵךְ בְּגֵיא צַלְמָוֶת לֹא־אִירָא רָע כִּי־אַתָּה עִמָּדִי שִׁבְטְךָ וּמִשְׁעַנְתֶּךָ הֵמָּה יְנַחֲמֻנִי׃	4	Even though I walk through the darkest valley, I will fear no evil, for you are with me; your rod and your staff, they comfort me.

3. **Identifying Conjunctions.** Use an interlinear Bible to discover what each of the bolded words are in Hebrew. All translations are from NIV unless otherwise noted.

	Verse	ו	כִּי	אִם	כִּי אִם	אוֹ	None
Ex.	**And** the word of Samuel came to all Israel. (1 Sam 4:1 ESV)	X					
a.	Then they will call to me **but** I will not answer. (Prov 1:28)						
b.	**For** the waywardness of the simple will kill them. (Prov 1:32a)						
c.	**and** the complacency of fools will destroy them. (Prov 1:32b)						
d.	**but** whoever listens to me will live in safety (Prov 1:33a)						
e.	**and** be at ease, without fear of harm. (Prov 1:33b)						
f.	**So** the priest gave him the consecrated bread. (1 Sam 21:6a [H7a])						
g.	**since** there was no bread there (1 Sam 21:6b [H7b])						
h.	**except** the bread of the Presence that had been removed . . . (1 Sam 21:6c [H7c])						
i.	**and** replaced by hot bread. (1 Sam 21:6d [H7d])						
j.	Don't you have a spear **or** a sword here? (1 Sam 21:8b [H9b])						

	Verse	ו	כִּי	אִם	כִּי אִם	אוֹ	None
k.	**If** any of them go outside your house into the street.... (Josh 2:19a)						
l.	their blood will be on our head **if** a hand is laid on them. (Josh 2:19f)						

4. **Interpreting ו cj.** Each item below contains a verse or part of a verse with at least one occurrence of the *waw* cj. For each passage below (1) use an interlinear Bible to count all the *waw* cjs in the complete verses cited below. (2) Then write the English translation(s) that represents the *waw* in the text quoted. If there is no English word to translate the Hebrew (note: there may be other ways, such as punctuation, to express the idea), write "None." (3) Identify the function based on the translation using the list in *HRU2*. Student answers may vary somewhat, but that's okay; translators disagree as well. There is at least one example of each of the categories listed in *HRU2*. All translations are from NIV unless otherwise noted.

	Verse	Freq	Word	Function
Ex.	In the beginning God created the heavens and the earth. (Gen 1:1)	1	and	Addition
a.	in life they were . . . admired, and in death they were not parted. (2 Sam 1:23b)			
b.	Now Boaz had gone up to the gate and sat down there. (Ruth 4:1 ESV)			
c.	her impurity is undetected (since there is no witness against her) (Num 5:13)			
d.	As long as the earth endures, seedtime and harvest, cold and heat, summer and winter, day and night will never cease. (Gen 8:22)			
e.	God called the light "day," and the darkness he called "night." (Gen 1:5a)			
f.	They shall wash their hands and feet so that they will not die. (Exod 30:21a)			
g.	Anyone who harms this man or his wife shall surely be put to death. (Gen 26:11b)			
h.	Oh, that their hearts would be inclined to fear me. (Deut 5:29)			
i.	No, my lord, but your servants have come to buy food. (Gen 42:10 NASB)			

(continued)

	Verse	Freq	Word	Function
j.	How can I go? If Saul hears about it, he will kill me. (1 Sam 16:2)			
k.	Walk with the wise and become wise, for a companion of fools suffers harm. (Prov 13:20)			
l.	Indeed, he blessed you. (Josh 24:10b ESV)			

5. **Interpreting כִּי.** For each passage below (1) use an interlinear Bible to identify which word in the English translation represents the כִּי. (2) Identify the function based on the translation using the list in *HRU2*. There is at least one example of each of the categories listed in *HRU2*. All translations are from the NIV unless otherwise indicated.

	Verse	Word	Function
Ex.	When the LORD your God brings you into the land he swore to your fathers, to Abraham, Isaac and Jacob, to give you—a land with large, flourishing cities you did not build (Deut 6:10)	When	Time
a.	If Cain is avenged seven times, then Lamech seventy-seven times. (Gen 4:24)		
b.	Then God blessed the seventh day and made it holy, because on it he rested from all the work of creating that he had done. (Gen 2:3)		
c.	And all Israel from Dan to Beersheba recognized that Samuel was attested as a prophet of the LORD. (1 Sam 3:20)		
d.	By the sweat of your brow you will eat your food until you return to the ground, since from it you were taken; for dust you are and to dust you will return. (Gen 3:19; two in this verse!)		
e.			
f.	Adam named his wife Eve, because she would become the mother of all the living. (Gen 3:20)		
g.	It was also called Mizpah, because he said, "May the LORD keep watch between you and me when we are away from each other." (Gen 31:49)		
h.	(and though Judah was the strongest of his brothers and a ruler came from him, the rights of the firstborn belonged to Joseph). (1 Chr 5:2)		
i.	The Levites even abandoned their pasturelands and property and came to Judah and Jerusalem, because Jeroboam and his sons had rejected them as priests of the LORD. (2 Chr 11:14)		
j.	He said to David, "Am I a dog, that you come at me with sticks?" And the Philistine cursed David by his gods. (1 Sam 17:43)		
k.	So then, it was not you who sent me here, but God. He made me father to Pharaoh, lord of his entire household and ruler of all Egypt. (Gen 45:8)		

6. **Flowcharting and Interpreting.** On a separate paper (use the form available on the *HRU* website mentioned in the introduction), as instructed in ch. 6, exercise 6, complete flowcharts for the following passages; if multiple versions are quoted, make a flowchart for each version. For now, do not bother with the functions of main clauses or prepositional phrases; focus on (a) coordinating conjunctions between clauses, (b) subordinating conjunctions at the beginning of clauses, and (c) on clauses without any introductory conjunction. Do this by labeling the function of each (a) coordinating conjunction, (b) subordinating conjunction, or (c) on the blank line before a clause that begins with no conjunction (you will have to figure out the function from reading the clauses). Be sure to answer any questions after each flowchart.

   a. Gen 8:21b

   Never again will I curse the ground because of humans, even though every inclination of the human heart is evil from childhood.

   I will never again curse the ground because of man, for the intention of man's heart is evil from his youth. (ESV)

   - Flowchart.
   - Where the NIV reads "even though," the ESV reads "for." Briefly explain the meaning of each translation. Use the labels for Hebrew prepositions provided in the corresponding chapter in *HRU2*.
   - Use an interlinear to identify the Hebrew conjunction in question. Write it down with the G/K and Strong's numbers.

   b. Judg 21:25

   In those days Israel had no king; everyone did as they saw fit.

   - Flowchart.
   - Notice that there is no conjunction. This means that the connection between the clauses is unmarked. Based on context, what do you think is the logical connection of the second clause to the first? The full range of choices is available, including no connection.

   c. 2 Kgs 17:7

   All this took place because the Israelites had sinned against the LORD their God.

   - Flowchart.
   - Copy the Hebrew word translated "because" and give the G/K and Strong's numbers.

   d. Num 9:10

   Tell the Israelites: "When any of you or your descendants are unclean because of a dead body or are away on a journey, they are still to celebrate the LORD's Passover."

Speak to the people of Israel, saying, If any one of you or of your descendants is unclean through touching a dead body, or is on a long journey, he shall still keep the Passover to the LORD. (ESV)

- Flowchart the NIV and label the function of each conjunction.
- Copy the Hebrew word translated "when" in the NIV and "If" in the ESV and give the G/K and Strong's numbers.
- Explain the difference in meaning between the two translations.

e. Ezek 44:10

But the Levites who went far from me, going astray from me after their idols when Israel went astray, shall bear their punishment.

- Flowchart the ESV and label the function of each conjunction.
- Briefly explain the meaning of the passage based on the grammar. In particular, quote the main clause; then list every phrase or clause that is a modifier and explain what it modifies.

f. Ezek 44:11–14

[11]They may serve in my sanctuary, having charge of the gates of the temple and serving in it; they may slaughter the burnt offerings and sacrifices for the people and stand before the people and serve them.

[12]But because they served them in the presence of their idols and made the people of Israel fall into sin, therefore I have sworn with uplifted hand that they must bear the consequences of their sin, declares the Sovereign LORD.

[13]They are not to come near to serve me as priests or come near any of my holy things or my most holy offerings; they must bear the shame of their detestable practices.

[14]And I will appoint them to guard the temple for all the work that is to be done in it.

- Flowchart the NIV and label the function of each conjunction.
- Based on the translation of conjunctions, which translation, NIV or NASB, is more formal?
- Explain any differences in interpretation resulting from differences in translation.

7. **Typing Practice.** Remember from ch. 1 that typing in Hebrew in the present day means that the program must be able to be bidirectional. MSWord does this amazingly well. Type out the answers you composed to the questions (not the flowcharts) for exercise 6 and include the relevant Hebrew words in your comment.

CHAPTER 8

LET'S NOT GET OURSELVES AHEAD OF

Prepositions

1. **Review.** If you wish, you may sing the *aleph bet* song as a refresher on the names of the letters. In the exercise below, write the Hebrew letters of the alphabet and their transliterations. Include the *begad-kepat* letters and final forms. Below each letter (L) write the transliteration (T).

															א	L
															ʾ	T
																L
																T

2. **Reading Practice.** Below is Ps 23:5–6 with the lines broken up at logical breaks. The NIV is provided in parallel.

תַּעֲרֹךְ לְפָנַי שֻׁלְחָן נֶגֶד צֹרְרָי דִּשַּׁנְתָּ בַשֶּׁמֶן רֹאשִׁי כּוֹסִי רְוָיָה:	5	You prepare a table before me in the presence of my enemies. You anoint my head with oil; my cup overflows.
אַךְ טוֹב וָחֶסֶד יִרְדְּפוּנִי כָּל יְמֵי חַיָּי וְשַׁבְתִּי בְּבֵית יְהוָה לְאֹרֶךְ יָמִים:	6	Surely your goodness and love will follow me all the days of my life, and I will dwell in the house of the LORD forever.

3. **Identifying Prepositional Phrases.** For each passage, copy the Pp, the word modified by the PPhr, and write the function of each PPhr using figure 8.2 in *HRU2*. The first one is done as an example. In this chapter, ignore the preposition *of*. This will be treated in ch. 11. All translations are from the NIV unless otherwise indicated.

	Prep.	Word Mod.	Function	Passage
Ex. 1 Ex. 2	because of because of	rejoice be happy	cause cause	I will rejoice because of the LORD; I will be happy because of the Lord who delivers me! (Hab 3:18 NET)
a. b.				Go from your country . . . to the land I will show you. (Gen 12:1)
c.				Serve him with wholehearted devotion. (1 Chr 28:9)
d.				The day of the LORD is near for all nations. (Obad 15)
e. f.				Yet I will wait patiently for the day of calamity to come on the nation invading us. (Hab 3:16)
g. h. i.				For if you remain silent at this time, relief and deliverance for the Jews will arise from another place. . . . (Esth 4:14)
j. k.				I will return to Jerusalem with mercy, and there my house will be rebuilt. (Zech 1:16)
l. m. n.				And I have promised to bring you up out of your misery in Egypt into the land of the Canaanites. (Exod 3:17)
o. p.				It [wisdom] is hidden from the eyes of every living thing, concealed even from the birds in the sky. (Job 28:21)

4. **Identifying Hebrew Prepositions and Functions.** The table below treats the same passages as in the previous exercise. Here the task is different. (1) In the first column write the **Hebrew** preposition represented by the bold-typed prepositions in the following verses. Use an interlinear Bible to identify the Hebrew. If you have a grammatically tagged computer Bible, it will give you that information. If you have a printed interlinear Bible, you will need to use Davidson to identify the preposition. *If there is no Hebrew preposition*, write "none" in the "Hebrew" column and do not complete the next two columns. (2) In the "English" column, write the **English** gloss most commonly found by using a word-study guide in a computer program or the *SNIVEC*. (3) Using the information in the list of Hebrew prepositions and function in *HRU2*, label the function of the preposition. The first one is done as an example. This might differ from what you labeled in the previous exercise.

	Hebrew	English	Function	Passage
Ex. 1 Ex. 2	בַּ בַּ	in in	cause cause	I will rejoice **because of** the LORD; I will be happy **because of** the Lord who delivers me! (Hab 3:18 NET)
a. b.				Go from your country . . . to the land I will show you. (Gen 12:1)
c.				Serve him **with** wholehearted devotion. (1 Chr 28:9)
d. e.				The day **of** the LORD is near **for** all nations. (Obad 15)
f. g.				The LORD, the God **of** heaven has given me all the kingdoms **of** the earth. (Ezra 1:2)
h. i. j.				Yet I will wait patiently **for** the day **of** calamity to come **on** the nation invading us. (Hab 3:16)
k. l. m.				For if you remain silent **at** this time, relief and deliverance **for** the Jews will arise **from** another place. . . . (Esth 4:14)
n. o.				I will return **to** Jerusalem **with** mercy, and there my house will be rebuilt. (Zech 1:16)
p. q. r. s.				And I have promised to bring you up **out of** your misery **in** Egypt **into** the land of the Canaanites. (Exod 3:17)
t. u. v. w.				It [wisdom] is hidden **from** the eyes **of** every living thing, concealed even **from** the birds in the sky. (Job 28:21)

CHAPTER 9

WHAT'S IN A NAME?
Overview of Nominals

1. **Reading Practice.** Below is the complete Ps 23 with the NIV in parallel. This time the Masoretic accents are included.

Hebrew	#	NIV
מִזְמוֹר לְדָוִד יְהוָה רֹעִי לֹא אֶחְסָר׃	1	*A psalm of David.* The Lord is my shepherd, I lack nothing.
בִּנְאוֹת דֶּשֶׁא יַרְבִּיצֵנִי עַל־מֵי מְנֻחוֹת יְנַהֲלֵנִי׃	2	He makes me lie down in green pastures, he leads me beside quiet waters,
נַפְשִׁי יְשׁוֹבֵב יַנְחֵנִי בְמַעְגְּלֵי־צֶדֶק לְמַעַן שְׁמוֹ׃	3	he refreshes my soul. He guides me along the right paths for his name's sake.
גַּם כִּי־אֵלֵךְ בְּגֵיא צַלְמָוֶת לֹא־אִירָא רָע כִּי־אַתָּה עִמָּדִי שִׁבְטְךָ וּמִשְׁעַנְתֶּךָ הֵמָּה יְנַחֲמֻנִי׃	4	Even though I walk through the darkest valley, I will fear no evil, for you are with me; your rod and your staff, they comfort me.
תַּעֲרֹךְ לְפָנַי | שֻׁלְחָן [a] נֶגֶד צֹרְרָי דִּשַּׁנְתָּ בַשֶּׁמֶן רֹאשִׁי כּוֹסִי רְוָיָה׃	5	You prepare a table before me in the presence of my enemies. You anoint my head with oil; my cup overflows.
אַךְ | טוֹב וָחֶסֶד יִרְדְּפוּנִי כָּל־יְמֵי חַיָּי וְשַׁבְתִּי בְּבֵית־יְהוָה לְאֹרֶךְ יָמִים׃	6	Surely your goodness and love will follow me all the days of my life, and I will dwell in the house of the Lord forever.

2. **Use of Number in Nominals.** By far the most common use of the singular and of the plural numbers is the numeric singular and plural. In the exercises below, I am going to give more examples of other uses than is commonly found. For each bold-type word in the following passages copy the Hebrew word as it appears in context (not the lemma or lexical form), indicate the gender and number of each noun. Based on context determine the use of the number in each version listed: if singular, write "numeric" or "collective"; if plural, write "numeric," "honorific," or "abstract." The first two are done as examples.

	Passage	Hebrew	G	N	Use of Number
Ex. 1	Let Us make **man** in Our image. (Gen 1:26 NASB;	אָדָם	m	s	Numeric
Ex. 2	cf. NIV **mankind**)				Collective
a.	In the image of God he created **him**. (Gen 1:27 ESV,				
b.	KJV; this is the sign of the DO with a PrnSf; cf. NIV, NET **them**).				
c.	See … the **oppression** among her people. (Amos 3:9 NIV; cf. NET **oppressive deeds**)				
d.	Behold … the **oppressed** in the midst thereof. (Amos 3:9, KJV; cf. ESV: See … the oppressed in her midst.)				
e.	Therefore hear, you nations; you who are **witnesses**, observe what will happen to them.				
f.	(Jer 6:18 NIV; cf. KJV **congregation**)				
g.	And I will put enmity between you and the woman, and between your **offspring** and hers. (Gen 3:15				
h.	NIV; cf. KJV **seed**)				
i.	I have been with **you** wherever you have gone. (2 Sam 7:9 NIV)				
j.	These he carried off to the temple of his **god** in Babylonia and put in the treasure house of his god. (Dan 1:2)				
k.	All the sailors were afraid and each cried out to his				
l.	own **god**. (Jonah 1:5 NIV; cf. NLT to their **gods**)				
m.	The **upright** love thee. (Song 1:4 KJV)				
n.	Rightly do they love you. (Song 1:4 ESV; cf. KJV note, **uprightly**)				

CHAPTER 10

BE SURE YOU READ THIS!

The Article

1. **Identifying Articles and Interrogatives.** Indicate which of the following words has the article (with or without the ה), the interrogative ה, or neither by writing an X in the appropriate column. Because you are not learning full Hebrew, you must use either a computer Bible with grammatical information of the Hebrew OT, or paper tools, such as John Owens, *Analytical Key to the Old Testament*, or Benjamin Davidson, *The Analytical Hebrew and Chaldee Lexicon*. The first one is done as an example.

	Passage	Word	Art.	Inter.	Neither
Ex.	Gen 1:1	הָאָ֫רֶץ	X		
a.	Gen 12:1	הַדְּבָרִים			
b.	Gen 14:24	הָלְכוּ			
c.	Gen 31:15	הֲלוֹא			
d.	Gen 1:25	הָאֲדָמָה			
e.	Gen 4:7	וּדְבַשׁ			
f.	Gen 17:17	הַלְּבֶן			
g.	Gen 17:17	הֲבַת			
h.	Gen 17:19	וַהֲקִמֹתִי			
i.	Gen 17:8	לֵאלֹהִים			
j.	Exod 22:9	לֵאֱלֹהִים			
k.	Ps 121:4	שׁוֹמֵר			

2. **Functions of the Presence of the Article.** Each bolded word in the passages below has the Hebrew article. Use the information in the chapter to identify the functions of the articles as interpreted by the translation. Answers may vary. At times verses are repeated using a different version. All the examples come from 1 Sam 1.

	Passage	Function
Ex. 1 Ex. 2	Once when they had finished eating and drinking in Shiloh, Hannah stood up. Now Eli **the priest** was sitting on **his chair** by the doorpost of the Lord's house. (1 Sam 1:9 NIV)	Anaphoric Pronominal
a.	And she said, "Let your servant find favor in your eyes." Then **the woman** went her way and ate. (1 Sam 1:18)	
b.	Early **the** next **morning** they arose and worshiped before the Lord. (1 Sam 1:19a)	
c.	and then went back to their home at **Ramah**. (1 Sam 1:19b)	
d.	So in the course of **time** Hannah became pregnant. (1 Sam 1:20)	
e.	**The man** Elkanah and all his house went up. (1 Sam 1:21 ESV)	
f.	When **her husband** Elkanah went up with all his family. (1 Sam 1:21a)	
g.	to offer **the annual**¹ sacrifice to the Lord and to fulfill his vow. (1 Sam 1:21b)	
h.	After **the boy** is weaned, I will take him. (1 Sam 1:22)	
i.	Elkanah her husband said to her, "Do **what seems best** to you. (1 Sam 1:23a ESV)	
j.	So **the woman** remained and nursed her son until she weaned him. (1 Sam 1:23b ESV)	
k.	And **the child** was young. (1 Sam 1:24d ESV)	
l.	Then they slaughtered **the bull**. (1 Sam 1:25a ESV)	
m.	and they brought **the child** to Eli. (1 Sam 1:25b ESV)	
n.	And she said to him, ". . . I am **the woman** who stood here beside you praying to the Lord." (1 Sam 1:26)	
o.	I am **the very woman** who stood here several years ago praying to the Lord. (1 Sam 1:26 NLT)	
p.	For **his** whole **life** he will be given over to the Lord. (1 Sam 1:28b)	

3. **Functions of the Absence of the Article.** Use the information in the chapter to identify the functions of the bolded anarthrous nouns as definite (D), indefinite (I), or qualitative (Q) by writing D, I, or Q in the DIQ column. If you identify the noun as definite, identify the function from the list of definite functions in the chapter as you did in the previous exercise by writing the function in the D Function column. Answers may vary. All the examples come from 1 Sam 1. I skip some nouns that would qualify.

---

1. Hint: literally, the Hebrew is "the days."

	Passage	DIQ	D Function
Ex. 1	There was **a** certain **man** from Ramathaim, a Zuphite from the hill country of Ephraim,	I	—
Ex. 2	whose name was **Elkanah**[2] son of Jeroham, the son of Elihu, the son of Tohu, the son of Zuph,	D	Identification
Ex. 3	**an Ephraimite.**[3] (1 Sam 1:1)	I	—
a.	He had two **wives**; (1 Sam 1:2a)		
b.	one was called **Hannah** and the other Peninnah. (1 Sam 1:2b)		
c.	Peninnah had **children**, but Hannah had none. (1 Sam 1:2c-d)		
d.	But Hannah had no **children**. (1 Sam 1:2d ESV)		
e.	**Year after year** [מִיָּמִים יָמִימָה][4] this man went up from his town to worship (1 Sam 1:3a)		
f.	and sacrifice to the Lᴏʀᴅ Almighty at Shiloh (1 Sam 1:3b)		
g.	where Hophni and Phinehas, the two sons of Eli, were **priests** of the Lᴏʀᴅ. (1 Sam 1:3c)		
h.	Whenever the day came for Elkanah to sacrifice, he would give **portions** of the meat to his wife Peninnah and to all her sons and daughters. (1 Sam 1:4)		
i.	But to Hannah he gave a double **portion** because he loved her, and the Lᴏʀᴅ had closed her womb. (1 Sam 1:5)		
j.	Because the Lᴏʀᴅ had closed Hannah's womb, her rival **kept provoking** her in order to irritate her. (1 Sam 1:6 NIV; cf. ESV "**grievously**," KJV "**sore**")[5]		
k.	This went on **year after year** [שָׁנָה בְשָׁנָה]. (1) Sam 1:7)		
l.	Her husband **Elkanah** would say to her, (1 Sam 1:8a)		
m.	**Hannah**, why are you weeping? (1 Sam 1:8b)		
n.	Don't I mean more to you than ten **sons**? (1 Sam 1:8e)		

---

2. Like English, proper nouns in Hebrew do not take the article (in Greek, they may). They are always definite, because they refer to a specific individual. So, all the proper nouns in the rest of this verse are also anarthrous and definite.

3. The final word, "an Ephraimite," is actually an adjective being used as a noun to identify the group of which Elkanah is a part, the Ephraimites (other interpretations have been put forth, of course).

4. The Hebrew is literally "from days days." *Days* is often used idiomatically to refer to a year. The repetition, "year year," is Hebrew idiom for an action repeated annually.

5. The NIV does not seem at first glance to translate this noun. The Hebrew clause would be literally, "And her rival used to anger her indeed to anger [גַּם־כַּעַס]" taking "anger" as an Adv Acc. It is good Hebrew idiom, of course, but it makes for awkward English. Evidently the translators thought that "kept provoking" was sufficient to get the meaning across, a meaning actually included in the verb (see ch. 15). More formal translations, such as the ESV and KJV, attempted to render the expression with an acceptable English equivalent that represents the Hebrew words present.

CHAPTER 11

A TALE OF TWO STATES
Case Functions

1. **Identifying Nom, Acc, and Voc Case Functions and Gen Object of Pp.** For Ezra 1:1–7, identify the case and function of the bolded word. If words are Gen Obj of Pp, include the Hebrew Pp. In this exercise, we will not include Prns included in or suffixed to verbs (see chs. 13–17). You will need to use an interlinear or other suitable resource. Unless indicated otherwise, the base version is NASB. Jeremiah 1:5 is done as an example.

	Passage	Word	Case	Function
Ex.	Before I formed thee in the **belly** I knew thee; and before thou camest forth out the **womb** I sanctified thee, *and* I ordained thee a **prophet** unto the **nations**. (Jeremiah 1:5 KJV)	belly womb prophet nations	Gen Gen Acc Gen	Obj Pp בְּ Obj Pp מִן Dbl Acc Person-Thing Obj Pp לְ
a.	Thus says **Cyrus king** of Persia, "The Lᴏʀᴅ, **the God** of heaven has given **me all** the kingdoms of the earth and **He** has appointed **me** to build **Him** a **house** in **Jerusalem**, which is in **Judah**. (Ezra 1:2)	Cyrus king The Lord the God me all He me Him house Jerusalem Judah		

(continued)

	Passage	Word	Case	Function
b.	**Whoever** there is among **you** of **all** His people, may **his God** be with **him**! Let him go up to **Jerusalem which** is in **Judah** and rebuild the **house** of the Lord, the God of Israel; **He** is the **God who** is in **Jerusalem**. (Ezra 1:3)	Whoever you all God him Jerusalem which Judah house He God who Jerusalem		
c.	**Every** survivor, at **whatever** place **he** may live, let the **men** of that place support him with **silver** and **gold**, with **goods** and **cattle**, together with a **freewill offering** for the **house** of God **which** is in **Jerusalem**." (Ezra 1:4)	Every whatever he men silver gold goods cattle fr. offer. house which Jerusalem		
d.	Then the **heads** of fathers' *households* of **Judah** and **Benjamin** and the **priests** and the **Levites** arose, even **everyone** whose **spirit** God had stirred to go up and rebuild the **house** of the Lord **which** is in **Jerusalem**. (Ezra 1:5)	heads Judah Benjamin priests Levites everyone spirit house which Jerusalem		

	Passage	Word	Case	Function
e.	**All** those about them encouraged them with **articles** of silver, with **gold**, with **goods**, with **cattle** and with **valuables**, aside from **all** that was given as a freewill offering. (Ezra 1:6)	All articles gold goods cattle valuables all		
f.	Also **King Cyrus** brought out the **articles** of the house of the Lord, **which Nebuchadnezzar** had carried away from **Jerusalem** and put in the **house** of his gods. (Ezra 1:7)	King Cyrus articles which Nebuchad. Jerusalem house		

2. **Identifying Genitive Constructions Based on Hebrew.** Use a computer Bible or other reference book to identify all the elements in the construct chains in Ezra 1:1–7. Do not include the sign of the DO, אֶת־, or chains of only two elements in which the preposition is N^h, or the infinitive construct (InfCst, ch. 17). Separate each element with a vertical stroke (|). Name the case of the N^h, except if it is a Pp. *Remember that possessive Prns suffixed to the end of a noun are genitives at the end of a chain*: "his book" = "the book of him," and can be marked thusly: his | book. The base version is NASB.

	Passage	Chain	Case N^h
Ex.	Now the sons of Israel again did evil in the sight of the Lord. So the Lord strengthened Eglon the king of Moab against Israel, because they had done evil in the sight of the Lord. (Judg 3:12)	sons of | Israel in | the sight of | the Lord the king of | Moab in | the sight of | the Lord	Nom — Acc —
a.	Thus says Cyrus king of Persia, "The Lord, the God of heaven has given me all the kingdoms of the earth and He has appointed me to build Him a house in Jerusalem, which is in Judah. (Ezra 1:2)		
b.	Whoever there is among you of all His people, may his God be with him! Let him go up to Jerusalem which is in Judah and rebuild the house of the Lord, the God of Israel; He is the God who is in Jerusalem. (Ezra 1:3)		

(continued)

	Passage	Chain	Case Nʰ
c.	Every survivor, at whatever place he may live, let the men of that place support him with silver and gold, with goods and cattle, together with a freewill offering for the house of God which is in Jerusalem." (Ezra 1:4)		
d.	Then the heads of fathers' *households*[1] of Judah and Benjamin and the priests and the Levites arose, even everyone whose spirit God had stirred to go up and rebuild the house of the Lᴏʀᴅ which is in Jerusalem. (Ezra 1:5)		
e.	All those about them encouraged them with articles of silver, with gold, with goods, with cattle and with valuables, aside from all that was given as a freewill offering.[2] (Ezra 1:6)		
f.	Also King Cyrus brought out the articles of the house of the Lᴏʀᴅ, which Nebuchadnezzar had carried away from Jerusalem and put in the house of his gods. (Ezra 1:7)		

3. **Determination.** For each bolded word in the passages below, place an X in the correct box to indicate whether it is determined by an article (Art), pronominal suffix (PrnSf), construct state with a determined noun (Cst),[3] lexical categories of proper noun or pronoun (Lex), or if it is undetermined (U). The passages are the same as in the previous exercise. Pronouns that are included in the verb (see ch. 13) are not bolded. For this exercise, the NASB is used.

	Passage	Art	PrnSf	Cst	Lex	U
Ex.	Now the **sons**			X		
	of **Israel** again did				X	
	evil	X				
	in the **sight**			X		
	of the Lᴏʀᴅ. So the Lᴏʀᴅ				X	
	strengthened **Eglon**				X	
	the **king** of			X		
	Moab				X	
	against **Israel**,				X	
	because they had done **evil**	X				
	in the sight of the Lᴏʀᴅ. (Judg 3:12)					

---

1. The word *households* is in italics in the NASB because there is not Hebrew word that it corresponds to; it is added for clarification. So, "fathers' households" represents one Hebrew word and "fathers'" is not the Gen after "households." Treat the entire phrase "fathers' households" as one word in your answer. To shorten the expression, omit "households." The NIV renders "family heads."

2. Hint: how many English words are used to translate the Hebrew word הִתְנַדֵּב?

3. This is actually identical to the noun with the PrnSf.

	Passage	Art	PrnSf	Cst	Lex	U
a.	Thus says **Cyrus** **king** of **Persia**, "The Lᴏʀᴅ, the **God** of **heaven** has given **me** all the **kingdoms** of the **earth** and **He** has appointed **me** to build **Him** a **house** in **Jerusalem**, which is in **Judah**. (Ezra 1:2)					
b.	Whoever there is among **you** of all **His** **people**, may his **God** be with **him**! Let him go up to **Jerusalem** which is in **Judah** and rebuild the **house** of the Lᴏʀᴅ, the **God** of **Israel**; **He** is the **God** who is in **Jerusalem**. (Ezra 1:3)					
c.	**Every** **survivor**, at **whatever** **place** he may live, let the **men** of **that** **place** support him with **silver** and **gold**, with **goods** and **cattle**, together with a **freewill offering** for the **house** of **God** which is in **Jerusalem**." (Ezra 1:4)					

(continued)

	Passage	Art	PrnSf	Cst	Lex	U
d.	Then the **heads** of **fathers'** *households* of **Judah** and **Benjamin** and the **priests** and the **Levites** arose, even **everyone**[4] **whose** **spirit** **God** had stirred to go up and rebuild the **house** of the LORD which is in **Jerusalem**. (Ezra 1:5)					
e.	**All** **those about** **them** encouraged **them** with **articles** of **silver**, with **gold**, with **goods**, with **cattle** and with **valuables**, aside from **all** **that was given as a freewill offering**.[5] (Ezra 1:6)					
f.	Also **King** **Cyrus** brought out the **articles** of the **house** of the LORD, **which** **Nebuchadnezzar** had carried away from **Jerusalem** and put in the **house** of **his** **gods**. (Ezra 1:7)					

---

4. The word כֹּל (*all, every*) is lexically determined. Most often it is in construct with a noun. In this case it is used absolutely without the Art.

5. This is an unusual construction. The Hebrew word rendered "the freewill offering" is actually an infinitive construct (InfC used absolutely; i.e., not in construct to a following word) used as a noun (see ch. 17). It does not have

4. **Genitive Functions.** All of the bolded terms are genitives. Identify the function using the functions from the chart in *HRU2*. Answers may vary and yield valuable discussion.

	Passage	Word Mod.	Gen Function
Ex.	[1] The vision of **Isaiah** the **son** of **Amoz** concerning **Judah** and **Jerusalem**, which he saw during **the reigns**[6] of **Uzziah**, **Jotham**, **Ahaz** and **Hezekiah**, **kings** of **Judah**. (Isa 1:1 NASB)	vision Isaiah son concerning concerning during reigns Uzziah, etc. kings	Possessor Simple Appos. Ancestor Obj of Pp עַל Obj of Pp עַל Obj of Pp בְּ Possessor Simple Appos. Ruled
a.	The **Israelites**[7] did evil in the **eyes** of the **Lord**; they forgot the **Lord their** God and served the Baals and the Asherahs. (Judg 3:7 NIV)		
b.	The anger of the **Lord** burned against **Israel** so that he sold them into the **hands** of **Cushan-Rishathaim** **king** of **Aram Naharaim**, to whom the Israelites were subject for eight years. (Judg 3:8 NIV)		
c.	When the sons of **Israel** cried to the **Lord**, the **Lord** raised up a deliverer for the **sons** of **Israel** to deliver them, Othniel the son of **Kenaz**, **Caleb's** younger brother. (Judg 3:9 NASB)		

(continued)

---

the Art, but it is extremely rare that an infinitive does have the Art (e.g., Jer 22:16; Ps 66:9; 121:3). Still, it may be taken as Det, being the Gen after כָּל.

6. Literally, "in the days of."

7. Check an interlinear Bible on this word to find out why it's labeled as having a Gen.

	Passage	Word Mod.	Gen Function
d.	The Spirit of the Lord came on **him**, so that he became **Israel's** judge and went to war. The Lord gave Cushan-Rishathaim king of **Aram** into the **hands** of **Othniel**, who overpowered him. (Judg 3:10 NIV)		
e.	So the land had peace for forty years, until Othniel son of **Kenaz** died. (Judg 3:11 NIV)		
f.	Oh, the blessings of **the man** who does not walk in the counsel of **the wicked** and in the path of **sinners** does not stand[8] and in the seat of **scoffers** does not sit! (Ps 1:1 author's translation)		
g.	but **whose** delight is in the law of the Lord, and who meditates on **his** law day and night. (Ps 1:2 NIV)		
h.	That person is like a tree planted by streams of **water**, which yields **its** fruit in season and **whose** leaf does not wither—whatever they do prospers. (Ps 1:3 NIV)		

5. **Case-Study Payoff.** Compare the versions of the following verses and answer the questions. Answers may vary and yield valuable discussion. If you are studying on your own, try to read a commentary that discusses the issue and "discuss" with the commentator.

   a. From that land he went *to Assyria* [אַשּׁוּר]. (Gen 10:11 NIV); the KJV reads "Out of that land went forth *Asshur*."

      i. Identify how each of these versions interpreted the case function of "Assyria" by naming the case and the function.

	Case		Function
NIV	Acc		Adv of Destination
KJV			

---

8. Hint: take "path" and "seat" as metaphors and as implying some action, walking (metaphorically for living) and sitting (metaphorically for judgment or leadership).

    ii. What difference is there in the understanding (check context to see who is the subject of the verb in the NIV)?

    iii. Take brief notes from a commentary or two to see how they treat this modifier (always cite your source).

b. I cried unto the LORD *with my voice* [קוֹלִי] (Ps 3:4 KJV). Compare the NIV84 rendering, "To the LORD I cry *aloud*."

    i. What is the case and function interpreted by each version?

	Case	Function
KJV		
NIV84		

    ii. What difference is there in the understanding?

c. We are considered *as sheep to be slaughtered* [כְּצֹאן טִבְחָה]. (Ps 44:22 NIV; literally, "as sheep of slaughter")

    i. Give the parsing information for each word.

Word	Lex	Stem	Form	P	G	N	State	Det	Case	Suff
as										
sheep										
slaughter										

Verbal Qualities: Lex, Stem, Form, P, G, N
Nominal Qualities: State, Det, Case, Suff

ii. What is the case and function of both nouns?

	Case	Function
sheep		
slaughter		

iii. Paraphrase "as sheep to be slaughtered" so that it clarifies the meaning for the reader based on the case and functions you identified. (Answers vary.)

d. And he had made him *a long robe with sleeves* [כְּתֹנֶת פַּסִּים]. (Gen 37:3 NRSV)

i. List the different ways each of the following versions[9] translates this clause and label the genitive function of each. Function labels should follow any English prepositions used. Place an X in the box "2-Trans" if the version double-translated the word translated as "sleeves" in the NRSV.

	Translation	Gen Function	2-Trans
NRSV, LEB	a long robe with sleeves		X
NIV			
NASB			
KJV, ASV			
ESV			
CSB, CJB			
Emph			
LES	a many-colored tunic	Attributive	
Message			
NET			
NCV			
NLT			
YLT			

9. CJB = Complete Jewish Bible; Emph = Emphasized Bible; LEB = Lexham English Bible; LES = Lexham English Septuagint; YLT = Young's Literal Translation.

ii. Complete the parsing chart below.

Word	Lex	Stem	Form	P	G	N	State	Det	Case	Suff
sleeves (NRSV)										

iii. Look up the Hebrew word for the word translated "sleeves" in a lexicon or the NET Bible notes. Taking into account all you've learned, what translation do you think best captures the meaning of the Hebrew? Why? Answers will vary.

e. *A Song of loves* [שִׁיר יְדִדֹת]. (Ps 45 title [Hebrew 45:1] KJV). Compare the NIV, "A *wedding* song"; ESV, "A *love* song."

i. What is the grammatical number of the Hebrew word behind "loves" (יְדִדֹת)?

☐ Singular   ☐ Plural

ii. Write the Gen function and numerical function (ch. 9) of יְדִדֹת as understood by each version.

	Gen Function	Numerical Function
KJV	Objective[10]	
NIV		
ESV		

f. *The fruit of the righteous* [פְּרִי־צַדִּיק] is *a tree of life* [עֵץ חַיִּים]. (Prov 11:30 NIV)

i. Both of these Gens are left unmarked. What do you think are the functions of each Gen noun?

Gen	Function
the righteous	
life	

10. Remember that translating the Gen with "of" is unmarked. Figuring out which Gen function is difficult here, because the meaning of "loves" is not clear, a frequent difficulty in interpreting the Psalm titles. If it means "types of love," then we might translate, "A Song *about* 'Kinds of' Love." "Loves" is then the object of the implied action of singing. If "loves" means something else, such as the name of a tune or song, it can be identified as a Gen of Apposition and might be paraphrased, "[the] song 'Loves'" or "the song which is 'Loves.'"

ii. Based on your function labels, how would you explain the meaning of this verse?

iii. Compare the NET translation: "The fruit of the righteous is like a tree producing life"; if you are interested, see the NET note.[11]

g. *My son* [בְּנִי], do not forget *my teaching* [תּוֹרָתִי]. (Prov 3:1 NIV)

Remember that a PrnSf is in the Gen case and means the same as "of me." The first "my" is possessor. Although you might be tempted to interpret the second "my" as possessor also, that is probably not the best answer. What is a good alternative? Think of how you would use a Gen case function to describe the "position" of the teaching between the teacher and the student.

Gen	Function
my teaching	

h. The LORD is *my shepherd* [רֹעִי], I lack nothing. (Ps 23:1 NIV)

i. Again, the "my" is not possessor; it is quite inappropriate to view the psalmist as the "possessor" of God. Be more precise.

Gen	Function
my shepherd	

ii. What devotional insight does this give you?

---

11. For a full treatment on the entire verse, see Lee M. Fields, "Proverbs 11:30: Soul-Winning or Wise Living?" *Journal of the Evangelical Theological Society* 50 (2007): 517–35.

i. I will establish *the throne of* his *kingdom* forever [כִּסֵּא מַמְלַכְתּוֹ]. (2 Sam 7:13 NIV)

    i. The NIV rendering does not specify a Gen function for "kingdom." Using information in this chapter, what do you think is the relation of "throne" to "kingdom"? The NLT translation reads: "And I will secure his *royal* throne forever."

Version	Gen	Function
NIV	the throne of his **kingdom**	
NLT	his **royal** throne	

    ii. How does the difference in perspective reflect on the meaning of the Hebrew expression? (Answers will vary.)

j. Now Abel was *a keeper of sheep* [רֹעֵה צֹאן], and Cain *a worker of the ground* [עֹבֵד אֲדָמָה]. (Gen 4:2 ESV) Compare the NIV, "Now Abel kept flocks, and Cain worked the soil."

    i. What function for both genitives did the NIV make precisely clear?

Version	Gen Function
NIV	

    ii. The ESV "of" leaves interpretation more the responsibility of the reader, while the NIV makes the meaning clearer. Which method do you prefer, or do you have different circumstances when either might be preferrable?

CHAPTER 12

AN APT DESCRIPTION
Adjectives

1. **Identifying Adjective Structures and Functions.** For each passage below (1) write the Adj (if there is no Adj, write "none" and go to the next verse). You will need to use a Hebrew interlinear, because sometimes Hebrew verbs are translated with English Adjs (see ch. 13) and for this exercise we need to find true Adjs. (2) Write the position (attributive, predicative, ambiguous, or isolated). (3) Mark "Y" in the Emph column if the Adj is emphasized and "N" if not. A maximum of one Adj is in each item.

	Passage	Adj	Function	Emph
Ex. 1	From the wilderness and this Lebanon, even as far as **the great river**, the river Euphrates, (Josh 1:4 NASB)	great	Attrib	N
Ex. 2	the river Euphrates, all the land of **the Hittites**, and as far as the Great Sea toward the setting of the sun will be your territory. (Josh 1:4 NASB)	Hittites	Isol	N
a.	The people served the Lord throughout the lifetime of Joshua (Judg 2:7a NIV)			
b.	and of the elders who outlived him (Judg 2:7b)			
c.	and who had seen all the great things the Lord had done for Israel. (Judg 2:7c)			
d.	Then the Israelites did evil in the eyes of the Lord and served the Baals. (Judg 2:11)			
e.	They forsook the Lord, the God of their ancestors. (Judg 2:12a)			
f.	They followed and worshiped various gods of the peoples around them. (Judg 2:12c)			
g.	They aroused the Lord's anger. (Judg 2:12d)			

(continued)

	Passage	Adj	Function	Emph
h.	A gazelle lies slain on your heights, Israel. (2 Sam 1:19a)			
i.	How the mighty have fallen! (2 Sam 1:19b)			
j.	Tell it not in Gath, proclaim it not in the streets of Ashkelon, lest the daughters of the Philistines be glad, lest the daughters of the uncircumcised rejoice. (2 Sam 1:20)			
k.	Your wickedness will punish you; your backsliding will rebuke you. (Jer 2:19a)			
l.	And know and see that your forsaking the Lord is evil (Jer 2:19b1 author's translation)			
m.	and bitter. (Jer 2:19b2, author's translation)			

2. **Identifying Relative Clauses.** For each passage below indicate (1) whether there is a relative pronoun (RP) present in both Hebrew (H) and English (E) by "Y" for Yes and "N" for No in the appropriate box, and (2) whether there is a relative clause (RC) present in both Hebrew (H) and English (E). You will need to use a Hebrew Bible or interlinear Hebrew Bible to complete this.

	Passage	RP H	RP E	RC H	RC E
Ex. 1	He also said to him, "I am the LORD, who brought you out of Ur of the Chaldeans to give you this land to take possession of it." (Gen 15:7 NIV)	Y	Y	Y	Y
Ex. 2	Ehud made himself a sword which had two edges, a cubit in length, and he bound it on his right thigh under his cloak. (Judg 3:16 NASB)	N	Y	N	Y
Ex. 3	*God* said to Abram, "Know for certain that your descendants will be strangers in a land that is not theirs . . . four hundred years. (Gen 15:13 NASB)	N	Y	Y	Y
a.	What is your name? (Gen 32:27 NIV)				
b.	He took them and sent them across the stream. And he sent across whatever he had. (Gen 32:23 NASB)				
c.	Now these are the names of the sons of Israel who came to Egypt with Jacob; they came each one with his household. (Exod 1:1 NASB)				
d.	The midwives, however, feared God and did not do what the king of Egypt had told them to do; they let the boys live. (Exod 1:17 NIV)				

	Passage	RP H	RP E	RC H	RC E
e.	But the midwives feared God, and did not do as the king of Egypt had commanded them, but let the boys live. (Exod 1:17 NASB)				
f.	Joseph died, and all his brothers and all that generation. (Exod 1:6 NASB)				
g.	"Do not come any closer," God said. "Take off your sandals, for the place where you are standing is holy ground." (Exod 3:5 NIV)				
h.	The Lᴏʀᴅ said, "I have indeed seen the misery of my people in Egypt. (Exod 3:7 NIV)				
i.	And now the cry of the Israelites has reached me, and I have seen the way the Egyptians are oppressing them. (Exod 3:9 NIV)				
j.	So now, go. I am sending you to Pharaoh to bring my people the Israelites out of Egypt. (Exod 3:10 NIV)				

3. **Analyzing Relative Clauses.** For the verses below, treat the RCs as we did in this chapter, except that here we will be supplying the information in the chart. *If there is a RC:* (1) in the RP column write "Y" for Yes or "N" for No; (2) in the "LW" column write the last word of the RC; (3–4) write the word that is the antecedent and in the "Function" column write "Descr," or if there is none, write "none" and the case function of the RC. Watch out, though; not all of these have RPs! *If there is no RC at all*, write "N" in every column.

	Passage	RP	LW	Antecedent	Function
Ex. 1	Now the Lᴏʀᴅ God had formed out of the ground all the wild animals and all the birds in the sky. He brought them to the man to see what he would name them; (Gen 2:19a NIV)	Y[1]	them	none	DO of *see*
Ex. 2	and whatever the man called each living creature, that was its name. (Gen 2:19b NIV)	Y	creature	none[2]	Nom Abs
Ex. 3	The Lᴏʀᴅ God fashioned into a woman the rib which he had taken from the man, and brought her to the man. (Gen 2:22 NASB)	Y	man	rib	Descr

(continued)

---

1. The English word "what" is a RPrn. The Hebrew is מָה, which is most often the interrogative "what?" It can also be used as a RPrn, usually indefinite, "what(ever)," as it is here.

2. The Hebrew is כֹּל אֲשֶׁר, literally, "all which." Technically the Hebrew RPrn has as its antecedent כֹּל, "all." English translations typically translate the two words idiomatically with an indefinite RPrn such as "whatever." The

	Passage	RP	LW	Antecedent	Function
a.	And this stone that I have set up as a pillar will be God's house, (Gen 28:22a NIV)				
b.	and of all that you give me I will give you a tenth. (Gen 28:22b NIV)				
c.	Abraham had taken another wife, whose name was Keturah. (Gen 25:1 NIV)				
d.	What is the matter, Hagar? (Gen 21:17 NIV)				
e.	He took them and sent them across the stream. And he sent across whatever he had. (Gen 32:23 NASB)				
f.	He also said to him, "I am the LORD, who brought you out of Ur of the Chaldeans to give you this land to take possession of it." (Gen 15:7 NIV)				
g.	(The gold of that land is good; aromatic resin and onyx are also there.) (Gen 2:12 NIV)				
h.	So Jacob and all his offspring went to Egypt, taking with them their livestock and the possessions they had acquired in Canaan. (Gen 46:6 NIV)				

4. **Flowcharting Practice.** Flowchart the following passages and briefly answer the questions below. For the keys to the flowcharts, see the end of the *Workbook*.

   a. Gen 8:21b

   Never again will I curse the ground because of humans, even though every inclination of the human heart is evil from childhood. (NIV)

   I will never again curse the ground because of man, for the intention of man's heart is evil from his youth. (ESV)

   i. Make two flowcharts of this passage, one based on the NIV and one on the ESV.

---

meaning is the same, but whereas the Hebrew RPrn has an antecedent, the English RPrn has no antecedent and functions as the object of the verb "called." More precisely, whatever is the complement of the double-accusative of person-thing (see ch. 11). Converting the RC to a main clause would yield, "The man called each living creature [DO; person] whatever [complement; thing]."

ii. Identify the Hebrew word rendered "even though" in the NIV. Look up the word in a wordbook or even use the information in *HRU2*, ch. 7, and give a brief note.

Hebrew Word:		Str:		G/K:	
Notes					

iii. Explain the difference between the way the two translations understand the two clauses. How does the second clause relate to the first?

iv. Concerning the Adj:

English word:		Hebrew word:	
Structure	☐ Attrib ☐ Pred ☐ Isol ☐ Ambig		
Emphasis?	☐ Y ☐ N		

b. 2 Sam 7:13
   i. Make a flowchart. The key is based on the NIV.
   ii. Check the context to identify the antecedent of "He."
   iii. How is he described?

c. Ruth 1:16
   i. Make a flowchart. The key is based on the NIV. Treat "where" as a RP.
   ii. What is the function of the "where" clauses?

d. Deut 6:4–9
   i. Make a flowchart. The key is based on the NIV. The "when" clauses are subordinate adverbial clauses introduced by a subordinating cj.
   ii. Are the English "when" clauses actually clauses (with a finite verb) in Hebrew (check an interlinear)?

      ☐ Yes   ☐ No

iii. Use an interlinear to look up v. 7. Explain the use of "and" in the "when" clauses in Hebrew, the NIV, and the NASB.

e. Zeph 3:12–13

    i.   Make a flowchart. The key is based on the NIV.

    ii. For review: Quote the verb with two accusatives and then quote the double accusative.

       1. Verb: _____

       2. Double Acc: _____ and _____

CHAPTER 13

WHERE THE ACTION IS

Overview of Verbals

1. **Reading Practice.** Below is Deut 6:4–5 with the lines broken up at logical breaks. The NIV is provided in parallel.

שְׁמַע יִשְׂרָאֵל יְהוָה אֱלֹהֵינוּ יְהוָה אֶחָד:	4	Hear, O Israel: The Lᴏʀᴅ our God, the Lᴏʀᴅ is one.
וְאָהַבְתָּ אֵת יְהוָה אֱלֹהֶיךָ בְּכָל־לְבָבְךָ וּבְכָל־נַפְשְׁךָ וּבְכָל־מְאֹדֶךָ:	5	Love the Lᴏʀᴅ your God with all your heart and with all your soul and with all your strength.

2. **Dynamic vs. Stative.** For each clause portion, taken from Isa 6, I give the translation. Indicate whether the Hebrew verb is stative or dynamic; the majority will be dynamic. The first one is done as an example.

	Vs.	Hebrew	NIV	Verb Type
Ex	1	וָאֶרְאֶה	I saw	dynamic
a.	2	יְכַסֶּה	they covered	
b.	2	יְעוֹפֵף	were flying	
c.	3	וְקָרָא	and they were calling	
d.	3	וְאָמַר	["and said" in ESV]	
e.	4	וַיָּנֻעוּ	shook	
f.	4	יִמָּלֵא	was filled	
g.	5	וָאֹמַר	I cried	

(continued)

	Vs.	Hebrew	NIV	Verb Type
h.	5	נִדְמֵיתִי	I am ruined	
i.	5	רָאוּ	have seen	
j.	6	וַיָּעָף	flew	
k.	6	לָקַח	he had taken	
l.	8	אֶשְׁלַח	shall I send	
m.	10	הַשְׁמֵן	Make	

3. **Stem and PGN Identification.** For each of the verbs in the chart below indicate the stem (G, N, D, Dp, H, Hp, HtD), person (1, 2, 3), gender (m, f, c), and number (s, p). Use a computer Bible or books as mentioned. The verses are all from Song 8.

	Vs.	NIV	Stem	P	G	N
Ex	1a	If only you **were** to me like a brother, who was nursed at my mother's breasts![1]	Q	3	m	s
a.	1b	Then, if **I found** you outside,				
b.	1c	**I would kiss** you,				
c.	1d	and no one **would despise** me.				
d.	2a	**I would lead** you				
e.	2b	and **bring** you to my mother's house—				
f.	2c	**she who has taught** me.				
g.	2d	**I would give** you spiced wine **to drink**, the nectar of my pomegranates.				
h.	3	His left arm is under my head and his right arm **embraces** me.				
i.	4a	Daughters of Jerusalem, **I charge** you:				
j.	4b	**Do** not **arouse**				
k.	4c	or **awaken** love				
l.	4d	until **it** so **desires**.				
m.	5a	Who is this **coming up** [Ptc] from the wilderness		—		

1. This is a very idiomatic expression in Hebrew. The "you" is not the Hebrew subject but is actually the DO of the verb. An attempt at a clumsily formal translation would be, "Who (or, If only [someone]) **would give** you to me as

	Vs.	NIV	Stem	P	G	N
n.	5b	**leaning** [Ptc] on her beloved?		—		
o.	5c	Under the apple tree **I roused** you,				
p.	5d	there your mother **conceived** you,				
q.	5e	there **she who was in labor** [= 1 word in Hebrew]				
r.	5f	**gave** you **birth**.				
s.	6a	**Place** me like a seal over your heart.				

4. **Second-Person Pronouns.** Remember that whereas modern English has one form for the second-person pronoun "you," Hebrew has four: ms, mp, fs, and fp. This is true for personal pronouns and verbs. For the same passage, give the GN for all the second-person Prns, whether from Prns or the verb (two participles are included as well).

	Vs.	NIV	G	N
Ex	1a	If only **you** were to me like a brother, who was nursed at my mother's breasts![2]	m	s
a.	1b	Then, if I found **you** outside,		
b.	1c	I would kiss **you**.		
c.	2a	I would lead **you**		
d.	2b	and bring **you** to my mother's house.		
e.	2d	I would give **you**[3] spiced wine to drink, the nectar of my pomegranates.		
f.	4a	Daughters of Jerusalem, I charge **you**:		
g.	4b	Do not arouse [subject of a command]		
h.	4c	or awaken love [subject of a command].		
i.	5a	Who is this **coming up** [Ptc] from the wilderness		
j.	5b	**leaning** [Ptc] on her beloved?		

(continued)

---

a brother." A grammatically tagged computer Bible gives all the grammatical information, even though it does not line up with the English grammar.

2. See the previous note. In addition, the English "who was nursed" is in Hebrew simply a noun, "suckling, nursing infant." Therefore, it was not treated separately for this exercise.

3. This PPrn is suffixed to the verb, which normally is the DO, and here it looks like the English IO. In Hebrew, the verb in the H-stem means "cause to drink" and the PrnSf is the DO.

	Vs.	NIV	G	N
k.	5c	Under the apple tree I roused **you**;		
l.	5d	there your mother conceived **you**,		
m.	5e	there she who was in labor gave **you** birth.		
n.	6a	Place me like a seal over **your** heart,		
o.	6b	like a seal on **your** arm.		

5. **Noting Word Order at Clause Beginnings.** Using a traditional interlinear Bible or computer program, indicate (1) whether the Hebrew clause begins with a *waw* conjunction, other conjunction, or no conjunction by writing "*waw*," "cj," or "—" in the Cj column, and (2) whether the clause begins with a verb or nonverb by writing "V" or "NV" in the "V/NV" column. For the narrative section of Gen 22, ignore direct speech, which I have put in italic type, and relative clauses, for which I have supplied the answer. Exodus 15 is a poem and is therefore direct speech of the author rather than reported direct speech of someone else by an author.

Gen 23:2	אַרְבַּע	בְּקִרְיַת	שָׂרָה	וַתָּמָת
	Arba	in Kiryath	Sarah	and (she) died

Ps 23:1	רֹעִי	·	יְהוָה
	my shepherd	(is)	the LORD

Ps 23:4d	עִמָּדִי	·	כִּי־אַתָּה
	with me	(are)	for you

	Vs.	NIV	Cj	V/NV
Ex. 1	Gen 23:2	She died at Kiriath Arba.	*waw*	V
Ex. 2	Ps 23:1	The LORD is my shepherd.	—	NV
Ex. 3	Ps 23:4d	For you are with me	cj	NV
a.	Gen 22:1b	He said to him, "*Abraham!*"		
b.	Gen 22:1c	"*Here I am,*" he replied.		
c.	Gen 22:2	Then God said, "*Take your son.*"		

Vs.		NIV	Cj	V/NV
d.	Gen 22:3a	Early the next morning Abraham got up		
e.	Gen 22:3b	and loaded his donkey.		
f.	Gen 22:3c	He took with him two of his servants and his son Isaac.		
g.	Gen 22:3d	When he had cut enough wood for the burnt offering,		
h.	Gen 22:3e	he set out [note: there are two verbs in Hebrew] for the place		
i.	Gen 22:3f	*God had told him about* [RC]	—	NV
j.	Exod 15:1a	Then Moses and the Israelites sang this song to the Lord		
k.	Exod 15:1b	: [NIV renders the Hebrew וַיֹּאמְרוּ לֵאמֹר with a colon; KJV has "and spake, saying"]		
l.	Exod 15:1c	I will sing to the Lord.		
m.	Exod 15:1d	for he is highly exalted.		
n.	Exod 15:1e	Both horse and driver he has hurled into the sea.		
o.	Exod 15:2a	The Lord is my strength and my defence;		
p.	Exod 15:2b	he has become my salvation.		
q.	Exod 15:2c	He is my God,		
r.	Exod 15:2d	and I will praise him,		
s.	Exod 15:2e	my father's God,		
t.	Exod 15:2f	and I will exalt him.		

6. **Flowcharting Main Clauses**. A flowchart of Judg 4:17–21 appears below with some annotations that you may find instructive. I have indented all subordinate clauses. The main clauses are kept far left, even in the indentations for direct speech. Using the categories from figures 13.9 and 13.10, write the function in the blank provided. The first one is done as an example. Note that direct discourse is indented 1 inch and bullets mark the beginning and ending of speech.

Main Clause Function	Vs	Judg 4:17-21 (NIV)

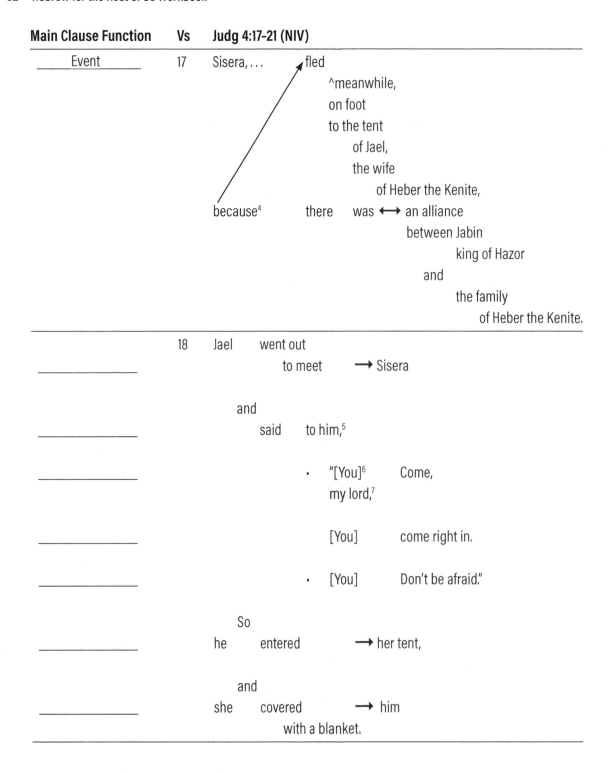

Event   17   Sisera, . . .   fled
                                              ^meanwhile,
                                              on foot
                                              to the tent
                                                  of Jael,
                                                  the wife
                                                      of Heber the Kenite,
                        because[4]   there   was ⟷ an alliance
                                                          between Jabin
                                                              king of Hazor
                                                          and
                                                              the family
                                                                  of Heber the Kenite.

                 18   Jael   went out
                                   to meet   → Sisera

                               and
                                   said   to him,[5]

                                       ·   "[You][6]   Come,
                                            my lord,[7]

                                            [You]   come right in.

                                       ·   [You]   Don't be afraid."

                               So
                               he   entered   → her tent,

                               and
                               she   covered   → him
                                        with a blanket.

---

4. The "because" clause should be indented under the verb "fled," but there is not room. The arrows indicate that this clause and the two PPhrs all modify the verb "fled."

5. After verbs of speaking and perceiving, the content of the speech or thought is the DO of the verb. "To him" is the IO of the verb and receives the speech. The IO stays on the main line.

6. Remember that all English commands have an implied *you* as the subject. I've added this to serve as a place holder for the subject.

7. Notice that, as usual, the vocative is appositional to the implied "you."

Main Clause Function	Vs	Judg 4:17–21 (NIV)
_____	19	.. "I'm thirsty,"
_____		he said.
_____		.. "[You] Please give me → some water."
_____		She opened → a skin of milk,
_____		gave him → a drink,
_____		and covered → him up.
_____	20	· [You] "Stand in the doorway · of the tent,"
_____		he told her.
_____ _____		· "If someone comes by
_____ _____		and asks you,
		.. 'Is anyone here?'
		· [You] say → · 'No.'" ·

(continued)

Main Clause Function	Vs	Judg 4:17-21 (NIV)

_____	21	But
		Jael,... picked up → a tent peg
		^Heber's wife,
		   and
		            → a hammer

_____		and
		    went
		      quietly
		      to him
		
		        while he lay fast asleep, exhausted.

_____		She drove → the peg
		        through his temple
		        into the ground,

_____		and he died.

CHAPTER 14

WHEN THE PERFECT COMES

Perfect Forms

1. **Reading Practice.** Below is Deut 6:6–7 with the lines broken up at logical breaks. Practice reading the Hebrew. The NIV is provided in parallel.

וְהָי֞וּ הַדְּבָרִ֣ים הָאֵ֔לֶּה אֲשֶׁ֨ר אָנֹכִ֧י מְצַוְּךָ֛ הַיּ֖וֹם עַל־לְבָבֶֽךָ׃	6	These commandments that I give you today are to be on your hearts.
וְשִׁנַּנְתָּ֣ם לְבָנֶ֔יךָ וְדִבַּרְתָּ֖ בָּ֑ם בְּשִׁבְתְּךָ֤ בְּבֵיתֶ֨ךָ֙ וּבְלֶכְתְּךָ֣ בַדֶּ֔רֶךְ וּֽבְשָׁכְבְּךָ֖ וּבְקוּמֶֽךָ׃	7	Impress them on your children. Talk about them when you sit at home and when you walk along the road, when you lie down and when you get up.

2. **Comparing Versions with the Hebrew.** In each of the following exercises the bolded verbs are either *qatal* or *weqatal* in Hebrew. (1) Use an interlinear Bible to identify the form, *qatal* or *weqatal* and check the appropriate box. (2) Use figures 13.9 and 13.10 to determine main clause function. (3 & 4) Use figure 14.6 and what you can gather from the context to determine the Tense Use and the Hebrew Verb Aspect of the action portrayed.

   Two notices: When you are analyzing main clause functions and aspects, you are figuring out how the English version translates the Hebrew, and then comparing it to the Hebrew functions that you've learned about here. Also, there is room for disagreement between readers. This is what makes studying the text together so valuable.

   (Ex.) Watch the field where the men are harvesting, **and follow along** after the women. **I have told** [cf. ESV, "**Have I** not **charged** . . . ?"] the men not to lay a hand on you. And **whenever you are thirsty, go and get a drink** from the water jars the men have filled. (Ruth 2:9 NIV)

Hebrew Form	Main Clause Function	Tense Use	Hebrew Verb Aspect
and follow along ☐ qatal ☒ weqatal	Command	Command	Constative
I have told ☒ qatal ☐ weqatal	NIV: Event	Perfect	Perfective
	ESV: Rhetorical question	Perfect	Perfective
whenever you are thirsty ☐ qatal ☒ weqatal	Habitual	Customary	Iterative
go ☐ qatal ☒ weqatal	Command, Permission	Command	Constative
get a drink ☐ qatal ☒ weqatal	Command, Permission	Command	Constative

a. That is why a man leaves his father and mother and **is united** to his wife, and they become one flesh. (Gen 2:24)

Compare the NET, "and **unites** with his wife"

Hebrew Form	Main Clause Function	Tense Use	Hebrew Aspect
☐ qatal ☐ weqatal	NIV:		
	NET:		

b. But **I will establish** my covenant with you, and **you will enter** the ark—you and your sons and your wife and your sons' wives with you. (Gen 6:18)

Hebrew Form	Main Clause Function	Tense Use	Hebrew Aspect
I will establish ☐ qatal ☐ weqatal			
you will enter ☐ qatal ☐ weqatal			

c. **I have set** my rainbow in the clouds, and it will be the sign of the covenant between me and the earth. (Gen 9:13)

Compare the KJV, "**I do set** my bow in the cloud."

Hebrew Form	Main Clause Function	Tense Use	Hebrew Aspect
☐ *qatal* ☐ *weqatal*	NIV:		
	KJV:		

d. Therefore, say to the Israelites: "I am the LORD, **and I will bring** you **out** from under the yoke of the Egyptians. I will free you from being slaves to them, and I will redeem you with an outstretched arm and with mighty acts of judgment." (Exod 6:6)

Hebrew Form	Main Clause Function	Tense Use	Hebrew Aspect
☐ *qatal* ☐ *weqatal*			

e. Whenever Moses went out to the tent, all the people would rise up, and each **would stand** at his tent door, and **watch** Moses until he had gone into the tent. (Exod 33:8 ESV)

    Compare the KJV, "all the people rose up and **stood . . .** and **looked**."

Hebrew Form	Main Clause Function	Tense Use	Hebrew Aspect
would stand ☐ *qatal* ☐ *weqatal*	ESV:		
	KJV:		
watch ☐ *qatal* ☐ *weqatal*	ESV:		
	KJV:		

f. Then Deborah said to Barak, "Go! This is the day the LORD **has given** Sisera into your hands. (Judg 4:14)

Hebrew Form	Main Clause Function	Tense Use	Hebrew Aspect
☐ *qatal* ☐ *weqatal*			

g. Whatever comes out of the door of my house to meet me when I return in triumph from the Ammonites will be the LORD's, **and I will sacrifice** it as a burnt offering. (Judg 11:31)

Hebrew Form	Main Clause Function	Tense Use	Hebrew Aspect
"and I will sacrifice": ☐ *qatal* ☐ *weqatal*			

h. His victims are crushed, they collapse; **they fall** under his strength.

He **says** to himself, "God **will never notice**; **he covers** his face **and never sees**." (Ps 10:10–11)

Compare NASB, "**and** the unfortunate **fall**. . . . **He says** to himself, "God **has forgotten**; He **has hidden** his face; **He will never see** it."

Hebrew Form	Main Clause Function		Tense Use	Hebrew Aspect
they fall ☐ qatal ☐ weqatal	NIV:			
	NASB:			
says ☐ qatal ☐ weqatal	NIV:			
	NASB:			
will never notice ☐ qatal ☐ weqatal	NIV:			
	NASB:			
he covers ☐ qatal ☐ weqatal	NIV:			
	NASB:			
and never sees ☐ qatal ☐ weqatal	NIV:			
	NASB:			

CHAPTER 15

THERE'S NOTHING WRONG WITH . . .

Imperfect Forms

1. **Reading Practice.** Below is Deut 6:8–9 with the lines broken up at logical breaks. The NIV is provided in parallel.[1]

וּקְשַׁרְתֶּם לְאוֹת עַל־יָדֶךָ וְהָיוּ לְטֹטָפֹת בֵּין עֵינֶיךָ׃	8	Tie them as symbols on your hands and bind them on your foreheads.
וּכְתַבְתָּם עַל־מְזוּזֹת בֵּיתֶךָ וּבִשְׁעָרֶיךָ׃ ס	9	Write them on the doorframes of your houses and on your gates.

2. **Comparing Versions with the Hebrew.** Follow the same procedure as in the ch. 14 exercises, but afterward, write a brief explanation about the differences in meaning of the versions.

   a. That is why a man **leaves** his father and mother and is united to his wife, and they become one flesh. (Gen 2:24)

   Cf. "For this reason a man **will leave**" (NIV84)

Hebrew Form	Clause Function	English Tense	Hebrew Aspect
leaves ☐ *qatal* ☐ *weqatal* ☐ *yiqtol* ☐ *wayyiqtol*	NIV: Assertion	Simple Past	Habitual
	NIV84: Anticipatory	Simple Present	Habitual
Explanation: (suggested answer) The NIV84 future tense might lead some to understand that this was a prediction of what would happen in the future. The NIV revision makes it clear that this is the norm of human behavior in marriage, and has been since the beginning.			

---

1. The ס at the end of v. 9 is a Masoretic abbreviation for the Aramaic word סתומא *sətûmā'*). Originally, of course, there were no paragraphs in the OT (or the NT for that matter). The chapter and verse numbering that we know in Bibles today was devised by Steven Langton in 1227 (see Norman L. Geisler and William E. Nix, *A General*

b. If **you make** an altar of stones for me, do not build it with dressed stones, for **you will defile** [cf. **you profane** (ESV)] it if **you use** a tool on it. (Exod 20:25 NIV)

Hebrew Form	Clause Function	English Tense	Hebrew Aspect
you make ☐ qatal ☐ weqatal ☐ yiqtol ☐ wayyiqtol	NIV:	NIV:	NIV:
you will defile ☐ qatal ☐ weqatal ☐ yiqtol ☐ wayyiqtol	NIV: ESV:	NIV: ESV:	NIV: ESV:
you use ☐ qatal ☐ weqatal ☐ yiqtol ☐ wayyiqtol			
Explanation:			

c. For the LORD your God is a merciful God; he **will** not abandon or destroy you or **forget** the covenant with your ancestors, which he confirmed to them by oath. (Deut 4:31 NIV)

Compare the NET, "he will not . . . destroy you, for **he cannot forget** the covenant"

Hebrew Form	Clause Function	English Tense	Hebrew Aspect
will . . . forget ☐ qatal ☐ weqatal ☐ yiqtol ☐ wayyiqtol	NIV: NET:	NIV: NET:	NIV: ESV:
Explanation:			

d. With persuasive words **she led** him **astray**; **she seduced** him with her smooth talk. (Prov 7:21 NIV)

Compare the ESV, "With much seductive speech **she persuades** him; with her smooth talk **she compels** him."

Introduction to the Bible, rev. and enl. ed. [Chicago: Moody Press, 1986], 340). Long before Langton the Hebrew Bible was divided into פְּסוּקִים (pəsûqîm), the basis for verses, and then into short paragraphs called *parashiyyoth* (פרשיות). The Masoretes marked these *parashiyyoth* as "open" (פְּתוּחָא [pətûḥāʾ] an Aramaic word abbreviated with a פ) or "closed" (סְתוּמָא [sətûmāʾ]). The pətûḥāʾ was the marker of larger sections. See Paul Joüon and T. Muraoka, *A Grammar of Biblical Hebrew*, rev. ed. (Roma: Pontificio Istituto Biblico, 2006), §116c, who use the Hebrew forms of the terms, and Page H. Kelley, Daniel S. Mynatt, and Timothy G. Crawford, *The Masorah of Biblia Hebraica Stuttgartensia: Introduction and Annotated Glossary* (Grand Rapids: Eerdmans, 1998), 155–56, under the entry ס.

Hebrew Form	Clause Function	English Tense	Hebrew Aspect
she led . . . astray ☐ qatal ☐ weqatal ☐ yiqtol ☐ wayyiqtol	NIV: ESV:	NIV: ESV:	NIV: ESV:
you use ☐ qatal ☐ weqatal ☐ yiqtol ☐ wayyiqtol	NIV: ESV:	NIV: ESV:	NIV: ESV:
Explanation:			

e. After that, the priest **must wash** his clothes and bathe himself with water. He **may** then **come** into the camp, but he will be ceremonially unclean till evening. (Num 19:7 NIV)

　　Compare the ESV, "Then the priest **shall wash**. . . . and afterward he may **come** into the camp. . . ."

Hebrew Form	Clause Function	English Tense	Hebrew Aspect
must wash ☐ qatal ☐ weqatal ☐ yiqtol ☐ wayyiqtol	NIV: ESV:	NIV: ESV:	NIV: ESV:
may come ☐ qatal ☐ weqatal ☐ yiqtol ☐ wayyiqtol	NIV: ESV:	NIV: ESV:	NIV: ESV:
Explanation:			

f. **We must take** a three-day journey into the wilderness to offer sacrifices to the LORD our God, as he commands us." (Exod 8:27 [Hebrew 8:23])

　　Compare the KJV, "**We will go** three days' journey into the wilderness."

Important to note here is the KJV use of "will." In 1611, the auxiliary verb "will" when used with the first person indicated more than just future time, but also desire or intentionality. This distinction is rarely maintained in modern, informal English.

Hebrew Form	Clause Function	English Tense	Hebrew Aspect
we must take ☐ qatal ☐ weqatal ☐ yiqtol ☐ wayyiqtol	NIV: KJV:	NIV: KJV:	NIV: KJV:
Explanation:			

g. The Israelites did so; they sent them outside the camp. **They did** just as the LORD **had instructed** Moses. (Num 5:4 NIV)

>   Compare the NASB: Just as the LORD **had spoken** to Moses, thus the sons of Israel **did**.

>   Explain which version follows the same order of verbs as the Hebrew.

Hebrew Form	Clause Function	English Tense	Hebrew Aspect
they did ☐ qatal ☐ weqatal ☐ yiqtol ☐ wayyiqtol	NIV & NASB:	NIV & NASB:	NIV & NASB:
had instructed ☐ qatal ☐ weqatal ☐ yiqtol ☐ wayyiqtol	NIV & NASB:	NIV & NASB:	NIV& NASB:
Explanation: Is there a devotional message that you can apply to yourself and present to others based on your explanation?			

h. Moses my servant **is dead**. (Josh 1:2 NIV)

Hebrew Form	Clause Function	English Tense	Hebrew Aspect
is dead ☐ qatal ☐ weqatal ☐ yiqtol ☐ wayyiqtol	NIV:	NIV:	NIV:

i. **I will give** you every place where **you set** your foot, as I promised Moses. (Josh 1:3 NIV)

>   Compare the NASB: "the sole of your foot **treads, I have given**."

>   Compare the ESV: "your foot **will tread** upon I have given."

Hebrew Form	Clause Function	English Tense	Hebrew Aspect
I will give ☐ qatal ☐ weqatal ☐ yiqtol ☐ wayyiqtol	NIV: NASB: ESV:	NIV: NASB: ESV:	NIV: NASB: ESV:
you set ☐ qatal ☐ weqatal ☐ yiqtol ☐ wayyiqtol	NIV: NASB: ESV:	NIV: NASB: ESV:	NIV: NASB: ESV:
Explanation:			

CHAPTER 16

WHERE THERE'S A WILL, THERE ARE . . .

Volitional Forms

1. **Reading Practice.** Below is Deut 6:4–9 with the lines broken up at logical breaks. The NIV is provided in parallel.

Hebrew	#	English
שְׁמַע יִשְׂרָאֵל יְהוָה אֱלֹהֵינוּ יְהוָה| אֶחָד׃	4	Hear, O Israel: The Lᴏʀᴅ our God, the Lᴏʀᴅ is one.
וְאָהַבְתָּ אֵת יְהוָה אֱלֹהֶיךָ בְּכָל־לְבָבְךָ וּבְכָל־נַפְשְׁךָ וּבְכָל־מְאֹדֶךָ׃	5	Love the Lᴏʀᴅ your God with all your heart and with all your soul and with all your strength.
וְהָיוּ הַדְּבָרִים הָאֵלֶּה אֲשֶׁר אָנֹכִי מְצַוְּךָ הַיּוֹם עַל־לְבָבֶךָ׃	6	These commandments that I give you today are to be on your hearts.
וְשִׁנַּנְתָּם לְבָנֶיךָ וְדִבַּרְתָּ בָּם בְּשִׁבְתְּךָ בְּבֵיתֶךָ וּבְלֶכְתְּךָ בַדֶּרֶךְ וּבְשָׁכְבְּךָ וּבְקוּמֶךָ׃	7	Impress them on your children. Talk about them when you sit at home and when you walk along the road, when you lie down and when you get up.
וּקְשַׁרְתָּם לְאוֹת עַל־יָדֶךָ וְהָיוּ לְטֹטָפֹת בֵּין עֵינֶיךָ׃	8	Tie them as symbols on your hands and bind them on your foreheads.
וּכְתַבְתָּם עַל־מְזוּזֹת בֵּיתֶךָ וּבִשְׁעָרֶיךָ׃ ס	9	Write them on the doorframes of your houses and on your gates.

2. **Volitional Forms.** For each form (1) use a grammatically tagged Hebrew Bible to identify the form as Imv, Coh, or Juss, and (2) use figure 16.4 and the translation and context to identify how the translation identifies the function. NIV is used, except when other versions are indicted.

	Passage	Verbal	Imv	Juss	Coh	Version	Function
Ex. 1	Exod 1:10	הָבָה	X			Come	Interjection
Ex. 2	Exod 1:10	נִתְחַכְּמָה			X	we must deal shrewdly	Resolve
Ex. 3						let us deal wisely (NASB)	Exhortation
a.	Exod 3:3	אָסֻרָה				I will go over	
b.	Exod 3:3	וְאֶרְאֶה				and see	
c.	Exod 3:5	שַׁל				Take off	
d.	Exod 3:18	נֵלְכָה־נָּא				Let us take	
e.	Exod 3:18	וְנִזְבְּחָה				to offer sacrifices	
f.	Deut 32:1	הַאֲזִינוּ				Listen	
g.	Deut 32:1	וַאֲדַבֵּרָה				and I will speak	
h.						and let me speak (NASB)	
i	Deut 32:38	יָקוּמוּ				Let them rise up	
j.	Deut 33:6	יְחִי				Let Reuben live	
k.	1 Kgs 2:20	תָּשֵׁב				"I have one small request to make of you," she said. "Do not refuse me."	

3. **Negatives with the Imp Forms.** For each example indicate whether the negative particle is general (לֹא) or specific (אַל). Then briefly explain why that negative particle was used.

	Passage	Text	אַל	לֹא	Significance
Ex. 1	Exod 2:3	**But when she could hide** him **no** longer	X		Suggested answer: Moses's mother would not be able to hide him anymore.
Ex. 2	Deut 33:6	Let Reuben live and **not die**		X	Suggested answer: The Lord declares that Reuben shall live at a future time. The "and not die" is specific to that time.
a.	Exod 3:3	why the bush **does not burn up**			
b.	Exod 3:5	**Do not come** any closer.			
c.	Exod 3:19	But I know that the king of Egypt **will not let** you go.			
d.	Deut 34:4	but **you will not cross over** into it			
e.	Deut 34:6	**But** to this day **no** one **knows** where his grave is.			
f.	Josh 1:5	**No** one **will be able to stand** against you all the days of your life.			
g.	Josh 1:7	Be strong and very courageous. Be careful to obey all the law my servant Moses gave you; **do not turn** from it to the right or to the left.			
h.	Josh 1:9	Have I not commanded you? Be strong and courageous. **Do not be afraid; do not be discouraged.**			
i.	Josh 1:18	Whoever rebels against your word and does not obey it, whatever you may command them, will be put to death.			

	Passage	Text	לֹא	אַל	Significance
j.	Ps 1:1	Blessed is the one who **does not walk** in step with the wicked or stand in the way that sinners take or sit in the company of mockers.			
k.	1 Kgs 2:20	"I have one small request to make of you," she said. "**Do not refuse** me."			

4. **Consecution of Tenses.** For each form (1) use a grammatically tagged Hebrew Bible to identify the form as Imv, Coh, or Juss, and (2) use figure 16.6 and the translation and context to identify how the translation identifies the function: as Independent-Sequential or as Dependent-Purpose.

	Passage	Text	V1	V2	V2 Function
Ex. 1	Exod 3:10	So now, **go** [V1]. **I am sending** [V2] you to Pharaoh.	Imv	וcj + Imp	Independent-Sequential
Ex. 2	Exod 3:10	**I am sending** [V1] you to Pharaoh **to bring** [V2] my people the Israelites out of Egypt.	וcj + Imp	ו + Imv	Dependent-Purpose
Ex. 3	Exod 3:16	**Go** [V1], **assemble** [V2] the elders.	Imv	וcj + Pf	Independent-Sequential
a.	Exod 3:18	**Let us take** [V1] a three-day journey . . . **to offer** [V2]			
b.	Deut 32:38	**Let them rise up** [V1] **to help you** [V2].			
c.	Deut 32: 49	**Go up** [V1] into the Abarim Range . . . **and view** [V2] Canaan.			
d.	Deut 32:50	**you will die** [V1] **and be gathered** [V2]			
e.		**Then die** [V1] . . . **and be gathered** [V2] (NASB)			
f.	Ps 2:3	**Let us break** [V1] their chains and **throw off** [V2] their shackles.			
g.	1 Kgs 2:17	Pease **ask** [V1] King Solomon . . . **to give** [V2] me Abishag.			
h.	Ps 4:4	**Tremble** [V1] and **do not sin** [V2].			
i.	Isa 1:18	**Come** [V1] now, **let us settle the matter** [V2].			
j.	Isa 2:3	**Come** [V1], **let us go up** [V2] to the mountain of the Lord, to the temple of the God of Jacob.			

	Passage	Text	V1	V2	V2 Function
k.	Isa 2:3	**Let us go up** [V1] to the mountain of the LORD, to the temple of the God of Jacob. **He will teach us** [V2] his ways.			
l.		**Let us go up** [V1] to the mountain of the LORD, . . .; **That He may teach us** [V2] concerning His ways. (NASB)			
m.	Isa 2:3	**He will teach us** [V1] his ways, so that we may walk [V2] in his paths.			
n.		**That He may teach us** [V1] concerning His ways **And that we may walk** [V2] in His paths. (NASB)			either![1]

---

1. For the NASB, both interpretations are possible. Does the clause "and that we may walk" depend on on "He may teach us" or on "let us go up"? What is the difference in meaning?

CHAPTER 17

TO INFINITIVES AND BEYOND!

Infinitives & Participles

1. **Reading Practice.** For the final two Reading Practices, we will read Jer 9:22–23 with the lines broken up at logical breaks. First the MT (see ch. 4) is given in transcription and transliteration. Then the NIV and NASB follow in parallel. In this section of Jeremiah, the Hebrew numbering includes the English 9:1 as 8:23, throwing off the numbering one verse. They reunite at 10:1. The texts below follow Hebrew numbering with Hebrew texts and English numbering with English texts. This is a nice verse to memorize. You might enjoy reading my series of blog posts on this from 2017.[1] In this lesson, we give just Jer 9:22 (English 23).

MASORETIC TEXT OF JER 9:22		
MT	**Vs**	**Transliteration**
כֹּה אָמַר יְהוָֹה	22a	*kō ʾāmar yəhwâ*
אַל־יִתְהַלֵּל חָכָם בְּחָכְמָתוֹ	b	*ʾal-yiṯhallēl ḥāḵām bəḥoḵmāṯô*
וְאַל־יִתְהַלֵּל הַגִּבּוֹר בִּגְבוּרָתוֹ	c	*wəʾal-yiṯhallēl haggibbôr biḡḇûrāṯô*
אַל־יִתְהַלֵּל עָשִׁיר בְּעָשְׁרוֹ׃	d	*ʾal-yiṯhallēl ʿāšîr bəʿošrô*

ENGLISH TRANSLATIONS OF JER 9:23		
NIV	**Vs**	**NASB**
This is what the Lᴏʀᴅ says:	23a	Thus says the Lᴏʀᴅ,
"Let not the wise boast of their wisdom	b	"Let not a wise man boast of his wisdom,
or the strong boast of their strength	c	and let not the mighty man boast of his might,
or the rich boast of their riches	d	let not a rich man boast of his riches

---

1. See part 1 (https://zondervanacademic.com/blog/something-to-brag-about-jeremiah-hebrew-and-you-lee-fields), part 2 (https://zondervanacademic.com/blog/something-to-brag-about-jeremiah-part-2-hebrew-and-you-lee-fields), and part 3 (https://zondervanacademic.com/blog/something-to-brag-about-jeremiah-922-23-part-3-articles-particles-and-verbals-oh-my-hebrew-and-you-with-lee-m-fields).

2. **Identifying Ptc and Inf functions.** For each translation given below, (1) indicate whether it is a Ptc, InfA, or InfC by placing a mark in the box, (2) and use figure 17.7 to identify the major function and any specific functions. For the examples and for Gen 43 the NASB is used; the NIV is used for Ezra 3.

	Passage	Verbal	English	Ptc	InfC	InfA	Function
Ex. 1	Gen 37:9 (NASB)	מִשְׁתַּחֲוִים	were bowing down	X			Verbal
Ex. 2	1 Sam 16:23	בִּהְיוֹת	whenever . . . came		X		Adv-Time
Ex. 3	Gen 37:8	הֲמָלֹךְ	[Are you] actually [going to reign over us?]			X	Adv-Emphasis of certainty
a.	Gen 43:2 (NASB)	לֶאֱכָל	Eating				
b.	Gen 43:3	הָעֵד	Solemnly				
c.	Gen 43:4	מְשַׁלֵּחַ	Send				
d.	Gen 43:6	לְהַגִּיד	by telling				
e.	Gen 43:7	שָׁאוֹל	Particularly				
f.	Gen 43:7	לֵאמֹר	Saying				
g.	Gen 43:7	הֲיָדוֹעַ	possibly (know)				
h.	Gen 43:12	הַמּוּשָׁב	that was returned				
i.	Gen 43:18	מוּבָאִים	are being brought in				
j.	Gen 43:18	לְהִתְגֹּלֵל	that he may seek				
k.	Ezra 3:5 (NIV)	הַמְקֻדָּשִׁים	the sacrifices				
l.	Ezra 3:6	לְהַעֲלוֹת	to offer				
m.	Ezra 3:7	לְהָבִיא	so that they would bring				
n.	Ezra 3:8	לְבוֹאָם	after their arrival				
o.	Ezra 3:8	הַבָּאִים	who had returned				
p.	Ezra 3:8	לְנַצֵּחַ	to supervise				
q.	Ezra 3:9	לְנַצֵּחַ	in supervising				
r.	Ezra 3:9	עֹשֵׂה	those working				
s.	Ezra 3:10	הַבֹּנִים	the builders				

	Passage	Verbal	English	Ptc	InfC	InfA	Function
t.	Ezra 3:10	מַלְבֻּשִׁים	in their vestments				
u.	Ezra 3:10	לְהַלֵּל	to praise				
v.	Ezra 3:11	בְּהַלֵּל	with praise				
w.	Ezra 3:11	בְּהַלֵּל	of praise				
x.	Ezra 3:12	בְּיָסְדוֹ	the foundation				
y.	Ezra 3:12	בֹּכִים	Wept				
z.	Ezra 3:12	לְהָרִים	shouted (aloud)[2]				

---

2. For this function, assume that the "wept" (בֹּכִים) is repeated from the previous clause.

CHAPTER 18

WHAT DO YOU MEAN?

Hebrew Word Studies

1. **Reading Practice.** Below are both verses of Jer 9:22–23 with the lines broken up at logical breaks. Again, the MT (see ch. 4) is given in transcription and transliteration following Hebrew numbering. Then the NIV and NASB follow in parallel following English verse numbering.

MASORETIC TEXT OF JER 9:22-23		
MT	**Vs**	**Transliteration**
כֹּה אָמַר יְהוָה	22a	kō ʾāmar yəhwâ
אַל־יִתְהַלֵּל חָכָם בְּחָכְמָתוֹ	b	ʾal-yiṯhallēl ḥāḵām bəḥoḵmāṯô
וְאַל־יִתְהַלֵּל הַגִּבּוֹר בִּגְבוּרָתוֹ	c	wəʾal-yiṯhallēl haggibbôr biḡbûrāṯô
אַל־יִתְהַלֵּל עָשִׁיר בְּעָשְׁרוֹ׃	d	ʾal-yiṯhallēl ʿāšîr bəʿošrô
	23a	kî ʾim-bəzōʾṯ yiṯhallēl hammiṯhallēl
הַשְׂכֵּל וְיָדֹעַ אוֹתִי	b	haśkēl wəyāḏōaʿ ʾôṯî
כִּי אֲנִי יְהוָה	c	kî ʾănî yəhwâ
עֹשֶׂה חֶסֶד מִשְׁפָּט וּצְדָקָה בָּאָרֶץ	d	ʿōśeh ḥeseḏ mišpāṭ ûṣəḏāqâ bāʾāreṣ
כִּי־בְאֵלֶּה חָפַצְתִּי	e	kî-bəʾēlleh ḥāp̄aṣtî
נְאֻם־יְהוָה׃	f	nəʾum-yəhwâ

ENGLISH TRANSLATIONS OF JER 9:23-24		
NIV	**Vs**	**NASB**
This is what the Lᴏʀᴅ says:	23a	Thus says the Lᴏʀᴅ,
"Let not the wise boast of their wisdom	b	"Let not a wise man boast of his wisdom,
or the strong boast of their strength	c	and let not the mighty man boast of his might,
or the rich boast of their riches,	d	let not a rich man boast of his riches;

(continued)

NIV	Vs	NASB
but let the one who boasts boast about this:	24a	but let him who boasts boast of this,
that they have the understanding to know me,	b	that he understands and knows Me,
that I am the Lord,	c	that I am the Lord
who exercises kindness, justice and righteousness on earth,	d	who exercises lovingkindness, justice and righteousness on earth;
for in these I delight,"	e	for I delight in these things,"
declares the Lord.	f	declares the Lord.

2. **Words of High Frequency.** A short cut strategy dealing with high frequency words is to limit searches to smaller samples, such as Psalms, or Isaiah, or the Minor Prophets. (No keys are provided for these. Answers to questions may vary.)

   a. And the Lord God formed man *of* the dust of the ground, and breathed into his nostrils the breath of life; and man became a living soul. (Gen 2:7 KJV)

      Question to answer: Does *soul* refer to that invisible, inner consciousness in man that distinguishes humans from animals? Limit your examination to Genesis; then add in Isaiah. What do you discover?

   b. Therefore the people of Israel shall keep the Sabbath, observing the Sabbath throughout their generations, as a covenant forever. (Exod 31:16 ESV)

      Question to answer: Does *forever* mean Christians should observe Sabbath laws today? Limit your search to Genesis–Deuteronomy.

   c. Hear, O Israel: The Lord our God, the Lord is one. (Deut 6:4)

      Question to answer: Does *one* mean that God is literally homogeneous and indistinguishable within himself, namely that God is not a Trinity? Limit your search to Deuteronomy.

   d. Should he return to her again? (Jer 3:1)

      Question to answer: This is a key term in Jeremiah. Determine a range of meaning for this word in the book of Jeremiah. Make a distinction between the different stems (in Logos, search a Hebrew Bible, such as the Lexham Hebrew Bible).

3. **Word Study Practice.** If you are working on a paper for another assignment, your teacher may let you choose a word for that assignment. Follow the procedure given in this chapter. A blank "Word-Study Guide" that you can use as a model is available in appendix 2 to *HRU2* or from the website mentioned in the introduction. (No keys are provided for these. Answers to questions may vary.)

   a. Then God said, "Let us make mankind in our image, in our *likeness*." (Gen 1:26)

      Question to answer: Do *image* and *likeness* mean that people were like God in full deity?

   b. I will make a helper suitable for him. (Gen 2:18)

      Question to answer: Does *helper* imply that Eve was a notch below Adam in status?

   c. There was a man in the land of Uz, whose name was Job; and that man was perfect and upright, and one that feared God, and eschewed evil. (Job 1:1 KJV)

      Question to answer: Was Job absolutely perfectly without sin? Do two-word studies: one on "perfect" and one on "upright."

    d. "Come now, and let us reason together," Says the Lord. (Isa 1:18 NASB)

        Question to answer: Is this a pleasant conversation between two friends?

    e. And Mizpah; for he said, The Lord watch between me and thee, when we are absent one from another. (Gen 31:49 KJV)

        Question to answer: Is this "watch" a prayer for God's care for the other person? To increase the number of passages, make a list of all the different words that come from the root and are found in Genesis–Deuteronomy.

    f. or sit in the company of mockers. (Ps 1:1)

        Question to answer: Study the word translated "mockers" by (1) identifying the root and (2) looking up all the occurrences of all the words that come from this root. (This is a manageable number of occurrences.)

    g. For thou wilt not leave my soul in hell; neither wilt thou suffer thine Holy One to see corruption. (Ps 16:10 KJV)

        Question to answer: Does this OT passage teach that Jesus went to actual hell (cf. Acts 2:31)?

4. **Optional Project.** If you are working on Josh 1, select two key words from the chapter, and perform a short-cut study on one word and a full study on the other. In both cases, be sure to explain how the results of your study helps you understand the passage.

CHAPTER 19

TOOLS OF THE TRADE
Books in Paper and Electronic Form

1. **Library building.** Take stock of your library by considering what you have and list three to five purchases you might make in the coming year.
   a. *Evaluate your personal library.* How many "Phase 1" books do you currently own? What books would you like to have to fill in some of the missing gaps? Do you have a Bible computer program?
   b. *Plan for future growth.* What Bible books do you plan on studying? What books would you like to add to your library? Make a gift list for Christmas or birthday.[1]

2. **Bibliography building.**
   a. *Consult one or more of the bibliographies presented in the chapter.* Take note of Bible books you want to study in the near future. This may be based on courses you will take or sermons or lessons you need to prepare.
   b. *Select five books you might like to have.* Select at least one reference book that would serve you broadly.
   c. *Consult a trusted person to advise you in your choices.* You might check with a minister or professor you know or is recommended to you.

---

1. For ideas, please see Lee M. Fields, *Hebrew for the Rest of Us*, 2nd ed. (Grand Rapids: Zondervan, 2023), ch. 19.

CHAPTER 20

IF IT'S NOT POETRY, IT'S . . .

Hebrew Prose

1. **Translating *Wayyiqtol* Forms.** The chart below lists the initial words of each narrative clause (i.e., it does not include embedded speech) for 1 Sam 16:21–23. Complete the chart below by giving the analysis for each Hebrew expression and compare the NIV and NASB translations. Use an interlinear Bible to gather the Hebrew and version information. Translations of Hebrew words that are inserted between the English words to render a given Hebrew expression are placed in [brackets]; untranslated words are marked with a long dash (—); and extra words that have no explicit counterpart in the Hebrew text are placed in {curly brackets}.

Vv.	Hebrew	Analysis	NIV	NASB
21a	וַיָּבֹא	1cs + Imp	[David] came	Then [David] came
21b	וַיַּעֲמֹד			
21c	וַיֶּאֱהָבֵהוּ			
21d	וַיְהִי			
22a	וַיִּשְׁלַח			
23a	וְהָיָה			
23b	וְלָקַח			
23c	וְנִגֵּן			
23d	וְרָוַח			
23e	וְסָרָה			

What do you think about the differences between the versions? Where does each version align with or deviate from the structure of the Hebrew?

2. **Flowcharting.** For each exercise complete a narrative flowchart of the passage indicated following the example in the chapter. Keys are available. Suggested keys for the flowcharts may be found at the conclusion of the *Workbook*.

    a. Prepare a flowchart of Gen 2:24–3:7. Is Gen 3:1 a good section break? What difference does it make? Read a good commentary and take notes on this matter.

    b. Prepare a flowchart of Josh 1:12–18. Look at Josh 1:1–18 in the NIV and note which verses begin new paragraphs. Then use an interlinear to look at the beginning of each paragraph. Where do you think the Hebrew author marks section breaks? Do you agree with the NIV? Compare paragraph divisions with another version (e.g., ESV).

    c. Prepare a flowchart of Isa 7:10–17. Compare the section titles in the NIV and ESV. Do you think vv. 10–17 belong to what precedes or with what follows? What are some observations from your flowchart that suggest how to understand the structure of the chapter?

    d. Prepare a flowchart of 1 Sam 16:14–17:1. How does the Hebrew mark the beginning of a new story? How does the NIV mark this beginning?

CHAPTER 21

IT MAY NOT RHYME, BUT IT'S STILL . . .

Hebrew Poetry

1. **Features of Poetry.** Use an interlinear to identify which poetic passages illustrate these five poetic features. Place a mark in the box that is the best example. Each answer is used once.

Feature	Job 3:8	Ps 111:3	Ps 147:3	Prov 12:1	Eccl 12:3
Alliteration					
Paronomasia					
Acrostic					
Terseness					
Imagery					

2. **Line Enumeration and Rhythm Count.** For the passage below, (a) assign line numbers based on the English version and following the guidelines in the chapter. For this exercise, do not merely label with successive letters, but apply numbering that reflects the structure of the verse. (b) In the final column, use an interlinear to give a count of the stressed syllables. Ignore the title; I give those numbers simply to serve as a model.

Psalm 15:1–5 (NIV)	Line	Count
A psalm of David.	0	2
¹ Lᴏʀᴅ, who may dwell in your sacred tent? Who may live on your holy mountain?		

² The one whose walk is blameless,
    who does what is righteous,
    who speaks the truth from their heart;		

Psalm 15:1–5 (NIV)	Line	Count

[3] whose tongue utters no slander,
    who does no wrong to a neighbor,
    and casts no slur on others;		

[4] who despises a vile person
    but honors those who fear the Lᴏʀᴅ;
who keeps an oath even when it hurts,
    and does not change their mind;		

[5] who lends money to the poor without interest;
    who does not accept a bribe against the innocent.
Whoever does these things
    will never be shaken.		

3. **Flowcharting.** Create a flowchart for each of the following passages and answer any questions. Suggested keys for the flowcharts may be found at the conclusion of the *Workbook*.

    a. The NASB marks Ps 55:1–3 as one stanza. Produce a flowchart for these verses using the techniques studied in this chapter including (a) line numbers, (b) hyphens (-) and equals signs (=) to join English words to reflect Hebrew word count by consulting an interlinear, (c) bold or other indicators to mark the verbs, (d) alignment of the parallel elements, retaining the NASB word order as much as possible, and (e) a count of stressed syllables. Below is v. 1 as an example; continue with vv. 2–3. **Note:** you may rearrange the English, if it helps you to count stressed syllabus.[1]

Vs	Elements	Ct
1a	**Give-ear-to** my-prayer, O God,	3
1b	**And-do=not=hide-Yourself** from-my-supplication;	2

    Then trace the logic of the cola using some form of the chart used in *HRU2*, ch. 21, and consulting figure 21.1.

    b. Ps 5:10 (NIV) reads:

        10a Declare them guilty, O God!
        10b Let their intrigues be their downfall.
        10c Banish them for their many sins,
        10d for they have rebelled against you.

---

1. For an extended illustration of how to do this and observations, please see the series beginning with Lee M. Fields, "'My God, my God, why have you forsaken me?' (Psalm 22:1–2): The Artful Hebrew Bible," *Hebrew and You* (blog), April 5, 2022, https://zondervanacademic.com/blog/psalm-22. As of this writing, the series is in progress and is expected to finish up in 2023.

The NIV has these lines arranged as two bicola (I've numbered cola with a simple succession of letters), even punctuating with a period after 10b. Follow the procedures from this chapter to determine if you agree with this punctuation. You will need to (1) identify the beginning and ending of the stanza in which v. 10 occurs (use the NASB); (2) create a poetry flowchart for those verses; (3) trace the logic of the lines; then (4) number the lines.

c. Take Ps 1 through the entire process explained in this chapter. Particularly, note the line counts. How many lines do you see in v. 4 after doing your line analysis? Do the lines give a clue as to how to outline the psalm? How does this help you appreciate the artfulness of Hebrew poetry?

d. Take a group of eight verses from Ps 119 through the entire process explained in this chapter. (Since this is an open-ended assignment, no key is provided.)

SUPPLEMENTAL HELPS

1. Keys to Reading Charts

2. Flowcharting Keys

1. Keys to Reading Charts[1]

Ch. 3, #1, Simple Vowels (Use as Key and for reading practice.)

								Letter
א ׳o	א, א ׳ā	א ׳a	א ׳ō	א ׳u	א ׳e	א ׳ē	א ׳i	aleph
בֹ bo	בָ, בּ bā	בַ ba	בֹּ bō	בֻ bu	בֶ be	בֵ bē	בִ bi	bet
גֹ ḡo	גָ, גּ ḡā	גַ ḡa	גֹּ ḡō	גֻ ḡu	גֶ ḡe	גֵ ḡē	גִ ḡi	gimel
דֹ do	דָ, דּ dā	דַ da	דֹּ dō	דֻ du	דֶ de	דֵ dē	דִ di	dalet
הֹ ho	הָ, הּ hā	הַ ha	הֹּ hō	הֻ hu	הֶ he	הֵ hē	הִ hi	he
וֹ wo	וָ, וּ wā	וַ wa	וֹ, וֹּ ô, wô	וּ[2] wwu	וֶ we	וֵ wē	וִ wi	waw

(continued)

---

1. Remember that you may access the audio-visual file on the Student Resources page for *Hebrew for the Rest of Us Workbook* at www.zondervanacademic.com.

2. The syllable וּ does not occur. When the *waw* is doubled, however, the *qibbuts* can occur, as in יְצַוֻּנִי, *yəṣaw | wu | nî*.

								Letter
zo	zā	za	zō	zu	ze	zē	zi	zayin
ḥo	ḥā	ḥa	ḥō	ḥu	ḥe	ḥē	ḥi	khet
ṭo	ṭā	ṭa	ṭō	ṭu	ṭe	ṭē	ṭi	tet
yo	yā	ya	yō	yu	ye	yē	yi	yod
ḵo	ḵā	ḵa	ḵō	ḵu	ḵe	ḵē	ḵi	kaph
lo	lā	la	lō	lu	le	lē	li	lamed
mo	mā	ma	mō	mu	me	mē	mi	mem
no	nā	na	nō	nu	ne	nē	ni	nun
so	sā	sa	sō	su	se	sē	si	samek
ʿo	ʿā	ʿa	ʿō	ʿu	ʿe	ʿē	ʿi	ayin
po	pā	pa	pō	pu	pe	pē	pi	pe
ṣo	ṣā	ṣa	ṣō	ṣu	ṣe	ṣē	ṣi	tsade
qo	qā	qa	qō	qu	qe	qē	qi	qoph
ro	rā	ra	rō	ru	re	rē	ri	resh
śo	śā	śa	śō	śu	śe	śē	śi	sin
šo	šā	ša	šō	šu	še	šē	ši	shin
to	tā	ta	tō	tu	te	tē	ti	tav

Ch. 4, #4, Composite Vowels (Use as Key and for reading practice.)

◌ִי	◌ֵי	◌ִי	◌וּ	◌וֹ	◌ֹה	◌ֶה	◌ֵה	◌ָה
אֵי 'ey	אֵי 'ê	אִי 'î	אוּ 'û	אוֹ 'ô	אֹה 'ōh	אֶה 'eh	אֵה 'ēh	אָה 'â
בֵּי bey	בֵּי bê	בִּי bî	בּוּ bû	בּוֹ bô	בֹּה bōh	בֶּה beh	בֵּה bēh	בָּה bâ
גֵּי gey	גֵּי gê	גִּי gî	גּוּ gû	גּוֹ gô	גֹּה gōh	גֶּה geh	גֵּה gēh	גָּה gâ
דֵּי dey	דֵּי dê	דִּי dî	דּוּ dû	דּוֹ dô	דֹּה dōh	דֶּה deh	דֵּה dēh	דָּה dâ
הֵי hey	הֵי hê	הִי hî	הוּ hû	הוֹ hô	הֹה hōh	הֶה heh	הֵה hēh	הָה hâ
וֵי wey	וֵי wê	וִי wî	ווּ wû [3]	ווֹ wô	וֹה wōh	וֶה weh	וֵה wēh	וָה wâ
זֵי zey	זֵי zê	זִי zî	זוּ zû	זוֹ zô	זֹה zōh	זֶה zeh	זֵה zēh	זָה zâ
חֵי ḥey	חֵי ḥê	חִי ḥî	חוּ ḥû	חוֹ ḥô	חֹה ḥōh	חֶה ḥeh	חֵה ḥēh	חָה ḥâ
טֵי ṭey	טֵי ṭê	טִי ṭî	טוּ ṭû	טוֹ ṭô	טֹה ṭōh	טֶה ṭeh	טֵה ṭēh	טָה ṭâ
יֵי yey	יֵי yê	יִי yî	יוּ yû	יוֹ yô	יֹה yōh	יֶה yeh	יֵה yēh	יָה yâ
כֵּי key	כֵּי kê	כִּי kî	כּוּ kû	כּוֹ kô	כֹּה kōh	כֶּה keh	כֵּה kēh	כָּה kâ
לֵי ley	לֵי lê	לִי lî	לוּ lû	לוֹ lô	לֹה lōh	לֶה leh	לֵה lēh	לָה lâ
מֵי mey	מֵי mê	מִי mî	מוּ mû	מוֹ mô	מֹה mōh	מֶה meh	מֵה mēh	מָה mâ
נֵי ney	נֵי nê	נִי nî	נוּ nû	נוֹ nô	נֹה nōh	נֶה neh	נֵה nēh	נָה nâ

(continued)

---

3. The consonantal *waw* can also be doubled in this combination: וּוּ, *-wwú* (e.g., Gen 27:29).

יֶ◌	יֵ◌	יִ◌	וֹ◌	וֹ◌	הֹ◌	הֶ◌	הֵ◌	הָ◌
סֵי sey	סֵי sê	סִי sî	סוּ sû	סוֹ sô	סֹה sōh	סֶה seh	סֵה sēh	סָה sâ
עֵי ʿey	עֵי ʿê	עִי ʿî	עוּ ʿû	עוֹ ʿô	עֹה ʿōh	עֶה ʿeh	עֵה ʿēh	עָה ʿâ
פֵּי pey	פֵּי pê	פִּי pî	פּוּ pû	פּוֹ pô	פֹּה pōh	פֶּה peh	פֵּה pēh	פָּה pâ
צֵי ṣey	צֵי ṣê	צִי ṣî	צוּ ṣû	צוֹ ṣô	צֹה ṣōh	צֶה ṣeh	צֵה ṣēh	צָה ṣâ
קֵי qey	קֵי qê	קִי qî	קוּ qû	קוֹ qô	קֹה qōh	קֶה qeh	קֵה qēh	קָה qâ
רֵי rey	רֵי rê	רִי rî	רוּ rû	רוֹ rô	רֹה rōh	רֶה reh	רֵה rēh	רָה râ
שֵׂי śey	שֵׂי śê	שִׂי śî	שׂוּ śû	שׂוֹ śô	שֹׂה śōh	שֶׂה śeh	שֵׂה śēh	שָׂה śâ
שֵׁי šey	שֵׁי šê	שִׁי šî	שׁוּ šû	שׁוֹ šô	שֹׁה šōh	שֶׁה šeh	שֵׁה šēh	שָׁה šâ
תֵּי tey	תֵּי tê	תִּי tî	תּוּ tû	תּוֹ tô	תֹּה tōh	תֶּה teh	תֵּה tēh	תָּה tâ

2. Flowcharting Keys

Ch. 6, Ex. 6 Keys

Beginning Flowcharting

a. I will break down the gate of Damascus. (Amos 1:5a)

Function	Vs	Amos 1:5a (NIV)			Ct
	5	I	will break down	→ the gate of Damascus	1

b. and I gave them to him. (Mal 2:5b)

Function	Vs	Mal 2:5b (NIV)			Ct
		and			1
	6	I	gave	→ them to him	

c. I gave you empty stomachs in every city. (Amos 4:6a)

Function	Vs	Amos 4:6a (NIV)			Ct
	6a	I gave you → empty stomachs in every city;			1

d. David took his men with him and . . . killed two hundred Philistines. (1 Sam 18:27a)

Function	Vs	1 Sam 18:27a (NIV)			Ct
	27	**David** took → his men[4] . . .			
		^and . . .			1
		^killed → two hundred Philistines.[5]			

2 Samuel 7:8c-16 (NASB)

e. [8] I took you from the pasture, from following the sheep, to be ruler over My people Israel.

Function	Vs	2 Sam 7:8c (NASB)			Ct
	8c	I took → you			
		from the pasture			
		from following → the sheep,			1
		to be[6] ↔ ruler			
		over my			
		people Israel.			

f. [9] I have been with you wherever you have gone and have cut off all your enemies from before you; and I will make you a great name, like the names of the great men who are on the earth.

Function	Vs	2 Sam 7:9 (NASB)			Ct
	9a	I have been ↔ with you			
	9b		wherever **you** have gone		5

(continued)

---

4. The ellipses (. . .) indicate that words are removed (or elided). The freestanding circumflex (^) marks words that were moved from the ellipsis.

5. This is a compound subject with a plural verb; it is a single clause.

6. This is an infinitive phrase, not a new clause; therefore, 8c is only one clause. Infinitives can have many functions, but one of the most common is purpose. If you're saying, "I want more now," please see ch. 17.

Function	Vs	2 Sam 7:9 (NASB)	Ct
	9c	and have cut off → all your enemies from before you;	
	9d I	and will make → you ↔ a great name, like the names of the great men	5
	9e	who are ↔ on the earth.	

g.   [10] I will also appoint a place for My people Israel and will plant them, that they may live in their own place and not be disturbed again, nor will the wicked afflict them any more as formerly, [11] even from the day that I commanded judges to be over My people Israel; and I will give you rest from all your enemies.

Function	Vs	2 Sam 7:10–11c (NASB)	Ct
	10a I	will also appoint → a place for My people Israel	
	10b	and will plant → them,	
	10c	that[7] they may live in their own place	
	10d	and not be disturbed again,	
	10e	nor will the wicked afflict → them any more as formerly,	7
	11a	[11] even from the day	
	11b	that[8] I commanded → judges to be ↔ over my people Israel;	
	11c I	and will give you → rest from all your enemies.	

7. This word "that" is the conjunction ו in Hebrew, and marks result here. On functions of *waw*, see ch. 7.

8. This word "that" is the relative pronoun (RPrn) אֲשֶׁר and introduces a subordinate clause. The arrow points to the antecedent. For more on relative clauses (RCs), see ch. 12.

h. The LORD also declares to you that the LORD will make a house for you.

Function	Vs	2 Sam 7:11d-e (NASB)					Ct
	11d	**The** LORD	also declares	to you			
	11e		that[9]	**the** LORD	will make	➝ a house for you.	2

i. [12] When your days are complete and you lie down with your fathers, I will raise up your descendant after you, who will come forth from you, and I will establish his kingdom.

Function	Vs	2 Sam 7:12 (NASB)				Ct
	12a	When	your **days**	are complete		
			and			
	12b		**you**	lie down	with your fathers,	
	12c	**I**	will raise up after you,	➝ your descendant		5
	12d		**who**	will come forth from you,		
			and			
	12e	**I**	will establish	➝ his kingdom.		

j. [13] He shall build a house for My name, and I will establish the throne of his kingdom forever.

Function	Vs	2 Sam 7:13 (NASB)			Ct
	13a	**He**	shall build for My name,	➝ a house	
			and		2
	13b	**I**	will establish of his kingdom forever.	➝ the throne	

---

9. This word "that" is the conjunction כִּי, for which see ch. 7, and introduces a subordinate clause that gives the content of the verb "declared." This entire clause functions as the DO of the verb and so I have marked it with an arrow (➝).

k. [14] I will be a father to him and he will be a son to Me; when he commits iniquity, I will correct him with the rod of men and the strokes of the sons of men, [15] but My lovingkindness shall not depart from him, as I took *it* away from Saul, whom I removed from before you.

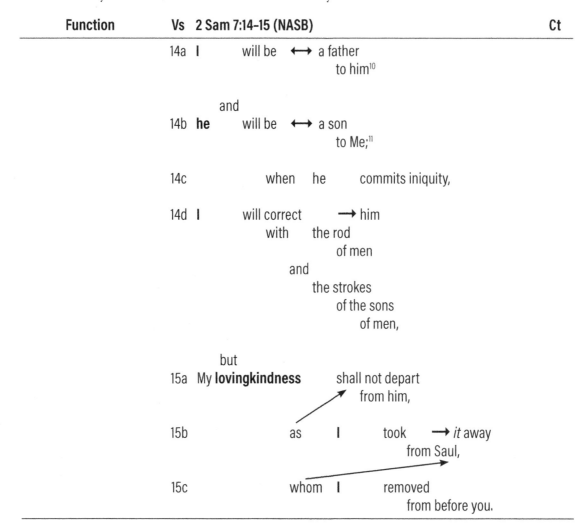

Function	Vs	2 Sam 7:14–15 (NASB)	Ct
	14a	I will be ↔ a father to him[10]	
		and	
	14b	**he** will be ↔ a son to Me;[11]	
	14c	when he commits iniquity,	
	14d	I will correct ⟶ him with the rod of men and the strokes of the sons of men,	
		but	
	15a	My **lovingkindness** shall not depart from him,	
	15b	as I took ⟶ *it* away from Saul,	
	15c	whom I removed from before you.	

l. [16] Your house and your kingdom shall endure before Me forever; your throne shall be established forever.

Function	Vs	2 Sam 7:16 (NASB)	Ct
	16a	Your house … shall endure ^and ^your kingdom before Me forever;	2
	16b	your throne shall be established forever.	

10. Another alternative to having "to him" modifying "father," in which case it is adjectival in function, is to have it modify the verb "will be," in which case it is adverbial. What is the meaning of each? Does Hebrew word order cause you to lean one direction more than another?

11. The phrase "to me" may be either adjectival, as I made it, or adverbial. Answer questions similar to those in n9.

Ch. 7, Ex. 6 Keys

a.   Gen 8:21b

> Never again will I curse the ground because of humans, even though every inclination of the human heart is evil from childhood (NIV)

> I will never again curse the ground because of man, for the intention of man's heart is evil from his youth. (ESV)

Function	Vs	Gen 8:21 (NIV)
	21	Never again will I curse ⟶ the ground because of humans,
Concession		even though every inclination ... is ⟷ evil ^of the human heart from childhood.

Function	Vs	Gen 8:21 (ESV)
	21	I will ... curse ⟶ the ground ^never again because of man,
Explanation		for the intention ... is ⟷ evil of man's heart from his youth.

- ○ Flowcharts
- ○ Where the NIV reads "even though," the ESV reads "for." Briefly explain the meaning of each translation. Use the labels for Hebrew prepositions provided in the chapter.

> NIV: The prediction/promise is given in spite of the fact that mankind is unchangeably evil.
> ESV: There are two coordinating clauses. The first is the same prediction/promise. The second gives the explanation, perhaps this: the ground will never be cursed, because mankind's nature is always bent toward sin and the ground does not deserve this treatment, or the cursing of the ground does not alter mankind's sinful tendencies.

- ○ Use an interlinear to identify the Hebrew conjunction in question. Copy the Hebrew word translated "because" and give the G/K and Strong's numbers.

> Hebrew: כִּי; G/K: 3954; Str: 3588

b. Judg 21:25

- Flowchart

Function	Vs	Judg 21:25 (NASB)
		In those days
	25	there was ⟷ no king
		in Israel
Result		Everyone did → [what was ⟷ right
		in his own eyes.][12]

- Notice that there is no conjunction. This means that the connection between the clauses is unmarked. Based on context, what do you think is the logical connection of the second clause to the first? The full range of choices is available, including no connection.

> Suggested answer (responses will vary): the second clause is Result, i.e., the consequence of having no king was anarchy and lawlessness.

c. 2 Kgs 17:7

All this took place because the Israelites had sinned against the Lord their God.

Function	Vs	2 Kgs 17:7 (NIV)
	7	All this took place
		↗
Cause		because the Israelites had sinned
		against the Lord their God.

- Flowchart
- Copy the Hebrew word translated "because" and give the G/K and Strong's numbers.

> Hebrew: כִּי; G/K: 3954; Str: 3588

d. Num 9:10

Tell the Israelites: "When any of you or your descendants are unclean because of a dead body or are away on a journey, they are still to celebrate the Lord's Passover."

- Flowchart the NIV and label the function of each conjunction.

---

12. Notice that the entire relative clause (RC; see ch. 12) is enclosed in brackets and the elements of the clause are spaced as any clause. There is no antecedent; the entire RC functions as the DO of the verb "did."

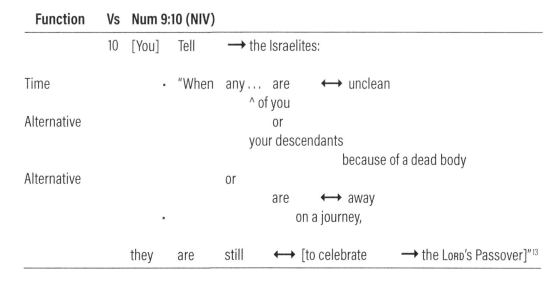

○ Copy the Hebrew word translated "when" in the NIV and "If" in the ESV and give the G/K and Strong's numbers.

Hebrew: כִּי; G/K: 3954; Str: 3588

○ Explain the difference in meaning between the two translations.

The NIV "when" may either be interpreted to be assuming that the Israelites will at some time or other become unclean, or it might be interpreted as when in general, without implying that they will. The ESV translation, "if," does not make the assumption that Israel will be unclean. Interpreters need to be careful about pushing language too rigidly.

e. Ezek 44:10

But the Levites who went far from me, going astray from me after their idols when Israel went astray, shall bear their punishment. (ESV)

○ Flowchart the ESV and label the function of each conjunction.

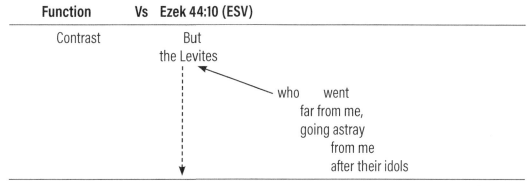

(continued)

---

13. The infinitive introduces a phrase, which I have placed in brackets, that functions as a noun, the predicate nominative (PN) of the verb "are." See ch. 17. Notice that the direct speech to the Israelites ("you") is a subordinate clause that breaks off without being complete and the missing main clause is found in the indirect speech of the final line.

Function	Vs	Ezek 44:10 (ESV)
Time		┆ when Israel went astray,
	10	└ - - - ► shall bear → their punishment.

- ○ Briefly explain the meaning of the passage based on the grammar. In particular, quote the main clause; then list every phrase or clause that is a modifier and explain what it modifies.

> The main clause is "But the Levites . . . shall bear their punishment." The subject, "the Levites," is modified by a relative clause, "who went." There are three adverbial modifiers of the verb "went": "far from me" = a **degree of separation** by the Levites from the Lord, "going astray" describing **how** they went, and "when Israel went away" giving the **time when** the Levites went away from the Lord.

f. Ezek 44:11–14

[11]They may serve in my sanctuary, having charge of the gates of the temple and serving in it; they may slaughter the burnt offerings and sacrifices for the people and stand before the people and serve them.

[12]But because they served them in the presence of their idols and made the people of Israel fall into sin, therefore I have sworn with uplifted hand that they must bear the consequences of their sin, declares the Sovereign LORD.

[13]They are not to come near to serve me as priests or come near any of my holy things or my most holy offerings; they must bear the shame of their detestable practices.

[14]And I will appoint them to guard the temple for all the work that is to be done in it.

- ○ Flowchart the NIV and label the function of each conjunction.

Function	Vs	Ezek 44:11-14 (NIV)
	11	They may serve
		in my sanctuary,
		having → charge
		of the gates
		of the temple
Addition		and
		serving
		in it;
		they may slaughter → the burnt offerings
Addition		and
		→ sacrifices
		for the people

Function	Vs	Ezek 44:11–14 (NIV)

Continuation   11   and
           stand
              before the people

Explanation   and
           serve → them.

     Contrast   But
Cause   because   they   served → them
                           in the presence
                             of their idols

Addition   and
                 made → the people … fall
                       ^of Israel
                           into sin,

Result   therefore
       12   I   have sworn
             with uplifted hand

Purpose   that   they   must bear → the consequences
                          of their sin,

       declares   the Sovereign LORD.

---

       13   They   are not   ↔ to come near
                         to serve → me
                         as priests
Alternative   or
                 ↔ come near → any
Alternative   of   my holy things
                             or
                     my most holy offerings;

       they   must bear → the shame
                     of their detestable practices.

     Continuation   And
       14   I   will appoint → them
             to guard   → the temple
             for all the work
                  that   is   ↔ to be done
                         in it.

○ Complete the chart below by checking the box to identify the Hebrew conjunction behind the English of the NIV (bolded with some following text for easy reference). In the final column, give the NASB translation of the conjunction alone.

Vs	NIV	וֹ	עַל־כֵּן	None	NASB
11	[untranslated] They	X			Yet
	and[1] serving	X			and
	and[2] sacrifices	X			and
	and[3] stand	X			and
	and[4] serve			X	[none]
12	But because			X	[none]
	and made	X			and
	therefore I have		X		therefore
	that they	X			that
13	[untranslated] They	X			And
	or[1] come	X			nor
	or[2] my most			X	nor
	[untranslated] they must	X			but
	[untranslated] of their	X			but
14	And I will	X			Yet

○ Based on the translation of conjunctions, which translation, NIV or NASB, is more formal?

NASB

○ Explain any differences in interpretation resulting from differences in translation.

1. Untranslated vs. "yet" in v. 11: the NIV does not define the relationship to the previous text, and it appears to be a member of a list including v. 10. The NASB "Yet" translates the Hebrew *waw* explicitly showing that there is a connection and clarifies that v. 11 is contrastive or concessive with v. 10: The Levites's sins are promised punishment in v. 11, but they will not be completely deleted from service.

2. In v. 11, the NIV adds "and[4]," implying that "standing before the people" and "serving" are parallel; the NASB uses the same form of Hebrew with "to serve" being an infinitive and indicating a subordinated idea to the standing.

3. Verse 12 begins with "But," making clear the interpretation that though the concession is made in v. 11 to allow Levites to serve in some ways, v. 12 reprises the limitation in v. 10. Neither the Hebrew nor the NASB specify the logical connection. The NIV's insertion seems correct, and the clarification is helpful.

4. Untranslated *waw* in v. 13 leaves the reader to figure out the existence of a connection to

the preceding. The NASB translates the *waw* "And." The *waw* connection seems to be an emphatic defining of the punishment from v. 10.

5. The or/nor variation between NIV and NASB has the same meaning.

6. Both the second untranslated *waw* and the NASB "but" leave the reader to determine the logical connection. "But" on the surface marks contrast; however, this is not marking contrast with the penalty in the first half of the verse, but is an emphatic detailing of the penalty.

7. For the final untranslated *waw* in v. 13, the NIV renders with a prepositional phrase, "the shame of their detestable practices"; this is a hyphenating use of the *waw*. The NASB "and" leaves the function unspecified; it might be simple addition, if the "shame" and the "abominations" are two separate items, but it might equal the NIV.

8. In v. 14 the NIV "And" leaves the function of the *waw* unspecified; the NASB "Yet" seems to mark a contrast from the last half of v. 13: that is, these Levites will be limited in their service, but they will be allowed to have a lower status roll.

Ch. 12, Ex. 4 Keys

a. Gen 8:21b

Never again will I curse the ground because of humans, even though every inclination of the human heart is evil from childhood.

I will never again curse the ground because of man, for the intention of man's heart is evil from his youth. (ESV)

Function	Vs	Gen 8:21b (NIV)
Time	21	Never again
Anticipatory		will I curse → the ground
Cause		because of humans,
Concession		← even though every inclination … is ↔ evil
Possessor		^of the human heart
Time		from childhood.

Function	Vs	Gen 8:21b (ESV)
Anticipatory	21	I will … curse → the ground
Time		^never again
Cause		because of man,
Explanation		for
Assertion		the intention … is ↔ evil
		from his youth.

b. 2 Sam 7:13

He is the one who will build a house for my Name, and I will establish the throne of his kingdom forever.

Function	Vs	2 Sam 7:13 (NIV)				
Assertion	13	He	is		⟷ the one	
Description				who	will build	→ a house
Beneficiary						for my Name,
Addition				and		
Anticipatory				I	will establish	→ the throne
Ruled						of his kingdom
Time (extent)					forever.	

c. Ruth 1:16

Function	Vs	Ruth 1:16 (NIV)					
Contrast	21	But					
Event		Ruth	replied,				
Command		.[14] "[You]	Don't urge		→ me	to leave[15]	→ you
Alternative (Command)						or	
						to turn back	
Separation						from you.	
Location				Where	you	go	
Anticipatory			I	will go,			
Addition				and			
Location				where	you	stay	
Anticipatory			I	will stay.			
Anticipatory			Your people	will be	⟷ my people		
Addition				and			
Anticipatory			your God		⟷ my God.		

14. I like to mark embedded speech with both an indent of the whole speech and a bullet at the beginning and ending of the speech. See ch. 13.

15. The expressions "to leave" and "to turn away" are both infinitives that complete the main verb and can be regarded as part of it (see ch. 17). So, I keep them on the same line as the main verb.

d. Deut 6:4–9

> [4] Hear, O Israel: The LORD our God, the LORD is one. [5] Love the LORD your God with all your heart and with all your soul and with all your strength. [6] These commandments that I give you today are to be on your hearts. [7] Impress them on your children. Talk about them when you sit at home and when you walk along the road, when you lie down and when you get up. [8] Tie them as symbols on your hands and bind them on your foreheads. [9] Write them on the doorframes of your houses and on your gates.

Function	Vs	Deut 6:4–9 (NIV)
Command	4	[You][16] Hear,
Address		O Israel:
Pending Nom		The LORD our God,
Assertion		the LORD is ⟷ one.
Command	5	[You] Love ⟶ the LORD
Acc of Apposition		your God
Means		with all your heart
Addition		and
Means		with all your soul
Addition		and
Means		with all your strength.
Assertion	6	These commandments . . . ⟷ are to be ⟷ on your hearts.[17]
Description		^that ⟶ I give you
Time		today
Command	7	[You] Impress ⟶ them
Destination		on your children.
Command		[You] Talk
Reference		about them
Time		when you sit
Location		at home

(continued)

Function	Vs	Deut 6:4–9 (NIV)		
Addition		and		
Time		when	you	walk
Location				along the road,
Time		when	you	lie down
Addition		and		
Time		when	you	get up.
Command	8	[You] Tie → them		
Purpose			as symbols	
Destination		on your hands		
Addition		and		
Command		[You] bind → them		
Destination		on your foreheads.		
Command	9	[You] Write → them		
Destination		on the doorframes		
Possessor		of your houses		
Addition		and		
Destination		on your gates.		

e. Zeph 3:12–13

> [12] But I will leave within you
>> the meek and humble.
>> The remnant of Israel
>> will trust in the name of the LORD.
> [13] They will do no wrong;
>> they will tell no lies.
>> A deceitful tongue
>> will not be found in their mouths.
>> They will eat and lie down
>> and no one will make them afraid.

Function	Vs	Zeph 3:12–13 (NIV)			
Contrast	·	But			
Anticipatory		I	will leave …	→ the meek	
Place			^within you		
Addition					and
DO 2	12			→ humble.	
Anticipatory		The remnant …	will trust		
Whole		^of Israel			
Specification			in the name		
Gen Apposition			of the Lord.		
Anticipatory		They	will do → no wrong;		
Anticipatory		they	will tell → no lies.		
Anticipatory		A deceitful tongue	will not be found		
Location			in their mouths.		
Anticipatory	13	They	will eat		
Addition		and			
Anticipatory			lie down		
Addition		and			
Anticipatory		no one	will make → them ↔ afraid."		

Ch. 20, #2, Flowchart Keys

a. Gen 2:24–3:7

Function	Vs	Passage: Gen 2:24–3:7 (NIV)	Clause Structure	Function
Assertion	24	That is why[18] a man leaves his father and mother	Cj + Imp	Inference Habitual
Assertion		and is united to his wife,	ו + Pf	Add Habitual
Assertion		and they become one flesh.	ו + Pf	Add Habitual
Event	25	Adam and his wife were both naked,	ו + Imp	Introductory
Event		and they felt no shame.	וַיֹּאמֶר + Imp	Concluding
Event	1	Now the serpent was more crafty	ו + NV	Initial
Comparison		than any of the wild animals	[PPhr]	[comparison]
Description		the LORD God had made.	RPrn	Past Pf
Event		He said to the woman,	וcs + Imp	Initiatory
Event		**"Did God really say,**	**Narrative**	**Informative**
Obligation		∷ **'You must not eat from any tree in the garden'→"**	**Hortatory**	**Persuasive**
Event	2	The woman said to the serpent,	וcs + Imp	Sequential
Permission		· **"We may eat fruit from the trees in the garden,**	**Expository**	**Informative**
Event	3	**but God did say,**	**Narrative**	**Informative**
Obligation		· **'You must not eat fruit from the tree**	**Hortatory**	**Persuasive**
Description		that is in the middle of the garden,		
Obligation		∷ **and you must not touch it, or you will die.'"**	**Hortatory**	**Persuasive**

16. The Hebrew for "That is why" is the compound preposition עַל־כֵּן. This makes the clause much easier to flowchart.

Function	Vs	Passage: Gen 2:24–3:7 (NIV)	Clause Structure	Function
Anticipatory Event	4	**"You will not certainly die,"** the serpent said to the woman.	**Predictive** ⌐CS + Imp	**Persuasive** Sequential
Assertion	5	**"For God knows . . .**	**Expository**	**Persuasive**
Time		**^when you eat from it**	—	
DO of *knows*		**^that . . . your eyes will be opened,**	—	
Anticipatory		**and you will be like God,**	**Predictive**	**Persuasive**
Description		**knowing good and evil."**		
Time	6	When the woman saw	⌐CS + Imp	Sequential
DO of *saw*		that the fruit of the tree was good for food and	—	
		pleasing to the eye,	—	
		and also desirable for gaining wisdom,	—	
Event		she took some	⌐CS + Imp	Sequential
Event		and ate it.	⌐CS + Imp	Sequential
Event		She also gave some to her husband,	⌐CS + Imp	Sequential
Description		who was with her,	—	
Event		and he ate it.	⌐CS + Imp	Sequential
Event	7	Then the eyes of both of them were opened,	⌐CS + Imp	Sequential
Event		and they realized	⌐CS + Imp	Sequential
DO of *realized*		they were naked;		
Event		so they sewed fig leaves together	⌐CS + Imp	Sequential
Event		and made coverings for themselves.	⌐CS + Imp	Sequential

b. Josh 1:12–18

Function	Vs	Passage: Josh 1:12–18 (NIV)	Clause Structure	Function
Event	12	But to the Reubenites, the Gadites and the half-tribe of Manasseh, Joshua said,		Contrastive
Imperative	13	• "Remember the command	ℸ + NV	Persuasive
Description		that Moses the servant of the Lord gave you after he said,	Hortatory	Informative
Anticipatory		· 'The Lord your God will give you rest	Predictive	Informative
Means		· by giving you this land.'	Expository	Informative
Permission	14	Your wives, your children and your livestock may stay in the land	Procedural	Informative
Description		that Moses gave you east of the Jordan,	Expository	—
Contrast		but	—	Persuasive
Obligation		all your fighting men, ready for battle, must cross over ahead of your fellow Israelites.	Hortatory	—
Obligation		You are to help them	—	Informative
Time	15	until the Lord gives them rest, as he has done for you,	Procedural	Informative
Time		and until they too have taken possession of the land	Predictive	Informative
Description		the Lord your God is giving them.	Predictive	Informative
Permission		After that, you may go back	Procedural	Informative
Permission		and occupy your own land,	Procedural	Persuasive
Description		which Moses the servant of the Lord gave you east of the Jordan toward the sunrise."	Narrative	
Event	16	Then they answered Joshua,	ℸcs + Imp	Sequential
DO of do		· "Whatever you have commanded us	—	—
Anticipatory		we will do,	Predictive	Performative
DO of go		and wherever you send us	—	—
Anticipatory		we will go.	Predictive	Performative

Passage: Josh 1:12-18 (NIV)

Function	Vs	Passage: Josh 1:12-18 (NIV)	Clause Structure	Function
Comparison	17	Just as we fully obeyed Moses,	Narrative	Performative
Anticipatory		so we will obey you.	Predictive	Relational
Wish		Only may the LORD your God be with you	Hortatory	
Comparison		as he was with Moses.	Narrative	
Subj of "put .."	18	Whoever rebels against your word	—	—
Subj of *put*		and does not obey it,	—	—
Description		whatever you may command them,	—	—
Anticipatory		will be put to death.	Predictive	Performative
Command		• Only be strong and courageous!"	Hortatory	Persuasive

c. Isa 7:10–17

Passage: Isa 7:10-17 (NIV)

Function	Vs	Passage: Isa 7:10-17 (NIV)	Clause Structure	Function
Event	10	Again the LORD spoke to Ahaz,	⌐cs + Imp	Initiatory
Command	11	• "Ask the LORD your God for a sign,	Hortatory	Persuasive
		• whether in the deepest depths	Hortatory	Persuasive
		or in the highest heights."	Hortatory	Persuasive
Event	12	But Ahaz said,	⌐cs + Imp	Sequential
Anticipatory		• "I will not ask;	Expository	Informative
Anticipatory		• I will not put the LORD to the test."	Expository	Informative

(continued)

Function	Vs	Passage: Isa 7:10-17 (NIV)	Clause Structure	Function
Event	13	Then Isaiah said,	Tcs + Imp	Sequential
Command		"Hear now,	Hortatory	Performative
Address		you house of David!	—	—
Assertion (RhQ)		Is it not enough to try the patience of humans →	Expository	Evaluative
Assertion (RhQ)		Will you try the patience of my God also →	Expository	Evaluative
Anticipatory	14	Therefore the Lord himself will give you a sign:	Predictive	Informative
Anticipatory		The virgin will conceive	Predictive	Informative
Anticipatory		and give birth to a son,	Predictive	Informative
Anticipatory		and will call him Immanuel.	Predictive	Informative
Anticipatory	15	He will be eating curds and honey	Predictive	Informative
Time		when he knows enough to reject the wrong and choose the right,	Predictive	Informative
Explanatory	16	for	—	—
Time		before the boy knows enough to reject the wrong	—	—
Time		and choose the right,	—	—
Anticipatory		the land of the two kings you dread will be laid waste.	Predictive	Informative
Anticipatory	17	The LORD will bring on you and on your people and on the house of your father a time unlike any	Predictive	Informative
Tims		since Ephraim broke away from Judah—	—	—
Anticipatory		he will bring the king of Assyria."	Predictive	Predictive

d. 1 Sam 16:14–17:1

Function	Vs	Passage: 1 Sam 16:14–17:1 (NIV)	Clause Structure	Function
Event	14	Now the Spirit of the LORD had departed from Saul,	ו + NV	Initial
Event		and an evil spirit from the LORD tormented him.	ו + NV	Parenthetic
Event	15	Saul's attendants said to him,	וcs + Imp	Initiatory
Assertion		**"See, an evil spirit from God is tormenting you.**	**Focusing**	**Evaluative**
Advice	16	**Let our lord command his servants here**	**Hortatory**	**Persuasive**
Complementary		**to search for someone**	—	—
Description		**who can play the lyre.**	—	—
Simple Future		**He will play**	**Predictive**	**Persuasive**
Time		**when the evil spirit from God comes on you,**	—	—
Simple Future		**and you will feel better."**	**Predictive**	**Persuasive**
Event	17	So Saul said to his attendants,	וcs + Imp	Sequential
Command		**"Find someone**	**Hortatory**	**Persuasive**
Description		**who plays well**	—	—
Command		**and bring him to me."**	**Hortatory**	**Persuasive**
Event	18	One of the servants answered,	וcs + Imp	Sequential
Event		**"I have seen a son of Jesse of Bethlehem**	**Narrative**	**Informative**
Description		**who knows how to play the lyre.**	—	—
Assertion		**He is a brave man and a warrior.**	**Expository**	**Persuasive**
Assertion		**He speaks well**	**Expository**	**Persuasive**
Assertion		**and is a fine-looking man.**	**Expository**	**Persuasive**
Assertion		**And the Lord is with him."**	**Expository**	**Persuasive**

(continued)

Function	Vs	Passage: 1 Sam 16:14–17:1 (NIV)	Clause Structure	Function
Event	19	Then Saul sent messengers to Jesse	וcs + Imp	Sequential
Event		and said,	וcs + Imp	Sequential
Command		• **"Send me your son David,**	**Hortatory**	**Persuasive**
Description		• **who is with the sheep."**	—	—
Event	20	So Jesse took a donkey loaded with bread,	וcs + Imp	Sequential
DO 2		a skin of wine and	—	—
DO 3		a young goat	—	—
Event		and sent them with his son David to Saul.	וcs + Imp	—
Event	21	David came to Saul	וcs + Imp	Sequential
Event		and entered his service.	וcs + Imp	Sequential
Event		Saul liked him very much,	וcs + Imp	Sequential
Event		and David became one of his armor-bearers.	וcs + Imp	Sequential
Event	22	Then Saul sent word to Jesse, saying,	וcs + Imp	Sequential
Command		• **"Allow David to remain in my service,**	**Hortatory**	**Persuasive**
Assertion		• **for I am pleased with him."**	Expository	Evaluative
Time	23	Whenever the spirit from God came on Saul,	וcs + Pf	Interative
Event		David would take up his lyre and play.	וcs + Pf	Interative
Event		Then relief would come to Saul;	וcs + Pf	Interative
Event		he would feel better,	וcs + Pf	Interative
Event		and the evil spirit would leave him.	וcs + Pf	Interative
Event	1	Now the Philistines gathered their forces for war	וcs + Imp	Introductory
Event		and assembled at Sokoh in Judah.	וcs + Imp	Complementary
Event		They pitched camp at Ephes Dammim, between Sokoh and Azekah.	וcs + Imp	Complementary

Ch. 21, #3, Flowchart Keys

Vs		Elements			Ct
1a	**Give-ear-to**	my-prayer,		O God,	3
1b	**And-do=not=hide-Yourself**	from-my-supplication.			2
2a	**Give-heed**	to me		**and-answer-me;**	3
2b	**I-am-restless**	in-my-complaint		**and-am-surely-distracted,**	3
3a1	Because-of-the-voice-of	the-enemy,			2
3a2	Because-of	the-pressure-of		the-wicked;	3
3b1	For=**they-bring-down**	trouble		upon-me	3
3b2	And-in-anger	**they-bear-a-grudge-against-me.**			2

a. Ps 55:1–3 (NASB)

	LOGIC		
Cola	**Logic**		
1a-b	Contrast: Base-Contrast	1ab-2ab: Synonymous. Base-Amplification	1ab-3b: Synthetic. Request-Cause
2a-b	Synthetic: Base-Cause		
3a1–2	Synonymous: General-Specific	3a-b: Synonymous. General-Specific	
3b1–2	Synonymous: Base-Amplification		

b. Ps 5:8–10 (NASB)

Vs		Elements			Ct
8a	O-Lord,	**lead-me**	in-Your-righteousness	because-of my-foes;	5
8b		**Make-straight**	Your-way	before me.	3
9a	There-is-nothing	reliable	in-what-they-say;		3
9b1	Their-inward-part [is]	destruction-*itself.*			2
9b2	Their-throat [is]	an=open=grave;			2
9b3	**They-flatter**	with-their-tongue.			2
10a1	**Hold-them-guilty,**	O God;			2
10a2	By-their-own-devices	**let-them-fall!**			2
10a3	In-the-multitude of	their-transgressions	**thrust-them-out,**		3
10b2	For=**they-are-rebellious**		against-You.		2

	LOGIC		
Cola	**Logic**		
8a–b	Synonymous: Base-Contrast		
9a	Monocolon	9a–b3: Synonymous General-Specific	8a/b–9a/10b: Synthetic: Reason-Request
9b1–2	Synonymous: Base-Restatement		
9b1/2–3	Synonymous: Base-Restatement		8a/b–9a/10b: Synthetic: Reason-Request
10a1–2	Synonymous: Base-Amplification	10a3–b: Synthetic Request-Reason	
10a1/2–3	Synonymous: Base-Amplification		
10b	Monocolon		

c. Ps 1:1–6 (NASB with adjusted word order to match the form of the Hebrew)

Vs	Elements				Ct
1a	How-blessed [is]	the-man	who		3
1b1	does not	walk	in-the-counsel-of	the-wicked,	4
1b2	Nor	in-the-path-of	sinners,	stand	4
1b3	Nor	sit	in-the-seat-of	scoffers!	4
2a	But (2)	his-delight-[is]	in-the-law-of	the LORD,	5
2b	And-in-His-law	he-meditates	day	and-night.	4
3a1	He-will-be	like-a-tree	*firmly*-planted	by=streams-of water,	5
3a2	Which	yields	its-fruit	in-its-season	4
3a3	And-its-leaf	does=not-wither;			2
3b	And-in-what	ever-he-does,	he prospers.		3
4a	The-wicked-[are]	not=so,			2
4b	But (2)=	they-are-like-chaff			3
4c	which-the-wind	drives-away.			2
5a	Therefore	the-wicked	will-not=stand	in-the-judgment,	4
5b	Nor-sinners	in-the-assembly-of	the-righteous.		3
6a	For=the-LORD	knows	the-way-of	the-righteous,	4
6b	But=the-way-of	the-wicked	will-perish.		3

LOGIC

Cola	Logic						
1a	Monocolon	1a–1b1/b3: Completion: Base-Content	1–2; Constrastive Base-Contrast	1/2–3a; Completion Base-Comparison	1a/3a3–3b Cause: Reason-Result	1/3–4/5; Contrast: Base-Contrast	1/5–6: Cause: Result-Reason
1b1–b2	Synonymous: Base-Restatement						
1b1/2–b3	Synonymous: Base-Restatement						
2a–b	Synonymous: Base-Amplification						
3a1–a2	Completion: Base-Attribution						
3a1/2–3a3	Completion: Base-Attribution						
3b	Monocolon						
4a	Monocolon	4a–4b/c: Completion: Base-Comparison	4–5; Cause: Reason-Result				
4b–c	Completion Base-Attribution						
5a–b	Synonymous: Base-Amplification						
6a–b	Contrast: Base-Contrast						

A note on the final column: remember that many of Wendland's logical pairs that do not include the term "base" may occur in either order. In my analysis, vv. 1–5 are all describing the positive outcome for the righteous and the negative outcome for the wicked. Verse 6 gives the reason for all this.